PROVIDENT:
A Centennial
History

PROVIDENT:
A Centennial
History

THE STORY OF

Provident Life and Accident

Insurance Company

BY

JOHN LONGWITH

PROVIDENT LIFE AND ACCIDENT
INSURANCE COMPANY
Chattanooga, Tennessee
1986

Library of Congress Catalog Number 86–082246
ISBN 0–9617768–0–3

Manufactured in the United States of America
by Arcata Graphics, Kingsport, Tennessee

ABOUT THE AUTHOR

John Longwith, a former teacher and law enforcement officer, was educated in the United States and England. He
writes for magazines and is the author of *Building to Last:
The Story of the American National Bank and Trust Company.* He is currently at work on a history of a Fortune-
500 manufacturer.

Contents

Foreword

This centennial volume represents the first time Provident has published a complete history. We deliberately chose for the author a professional writer of business history, who was not previously associated with the company, because we thought it valuable to secure an objective point of view.

John Longwith has had access to our full range of documents and other records, and he also conducted extensive interviews with many veteran Provident associates from the home office and field offices. Inevitably, there will be differences of memory and opinion about some events, but a variety of viewpoints is also part of our heritage.

After a rather inauspicious beginning, Provident has weathered two World Wars, the Great Depression, and all the social, political and technological changes of the past 100 years. There is a sturdy sense of self about this company which has enabled us in every era not only to survive, but also to grow and reach out for new challenges.

We hope this history will bring new insights to readers both inside and outside the company. We are certain it will illuminate some of the reasons why we have grown to become the leading company we are today.

HUGH O. MACLELLAN
Chairman, Finance
   Committee

H. CAREY HANLIN
President and
Chief Executive Officer

Preface

This book is an official history of the Provident Life and Accident Insurance Company. In dealing with the vast array of historical material created by so large and complex an organization, I have tried to keep myself, and the reader, from becoming lost in the backroads of endless detail. I have, therefore, focused on landmarks and left the job of naming every detour and milepost to Provident's internal publications.

I could not have completed my task without the cooperation of dozens of persons who consented to interviews or who otherwise affected the contents of this book. I am grateful to those who generously shared with me their recollections of Provident: James Althaus, Daisy M. Anderson, Todd Baker, Dr. William R. Bishop, Tom Bond, J. Robert Bracewell, Charles Cady, Alice Call, John Campbell, Mrs. William C. Cartinhour, Jac Chambliss, John O. Carter, Jr., Brooks Chandler, Attis Crowe, John Dail, Lafayette Davis, G. N. Dickinson, Jr., Carl Dyer, Frank Fitzgerald, David J. Fridl, Leland T. Fussell, Marshall Goodmanson, Robert Gordon, Charles Griffith, H. Carey Hanlin, Ernestine Hinds, Sam Holloway, Kathy Ingle, Dean Jackson, Vernon (Jim) Johnson, Al Jones, William L. Jones, Mrs. J. W. Kirksey, Jr., and Ada Parks Krug.

And also: Juanita Ledford, Mr. and Mrs. Hugh Owen Maclellan, Hugh O. Maclellan, Jr., Mrs. Robert L. Maclellan, Jewell Manning, Sam E. Miles, Edward L. Mitchell, Earl Montgomery, James H. Nelson, M. C. (Joe) Nichols, David N. Parks, Shirley Pecktol, Dudley

Porter, Jr., James E. Powell, Jr., Robert A. Reno, Louise Richardson, B. E. Ridge, Jr., Mrs. Betty Kirksey Scott, James W. Sedgwick, Don Simon, Floyd Smith, Ron Smith, John Starbuck, Lamar Stone, Henry Unruh, John H. Van Wickler, Thelma Washburn, John W. Wesley, Eston V. Whelchel, George Willis, John K. Witherspoon and Willard H. Wyeth.

Others deserve special mention. Among them are Mr. and Mrs. Hugh O. Maclellan, who allowed me access to many of Thomas Maclellan's early letters.

Mike Bishop, vice president of Corporate Communications, worked with me from the start, providing valuable advice and editing the original manuscript. His staff also pitched in to help, and though all cannot be named, some should be singled out for mention: Jennie Storey, Jeannine Mitchell, Gwen Moore and Lee Heidel.

Those outside Provident who contributed information and insight for which I am particularly grateful are William G. Brown, of the American National Bank and Trust Company; John Hartline, of the Norfolk-Southern Railroad; James Oaks, of the Seaboard System Railroad; and Professor Ronald D. Eller, whose *Miners, Millhands, and Mountaineers* re-created for me the historical backdrop against which Provident's early development unfolded.

Thanks also go to Dr. Robert Lanza, for proofreading the manuscript; and to the Chattanooga-Hamilton County Bicentennial Library, whose remarkable Local History Collection often held just the document that I could find nowhere else.

June 1986   J. L.

1

Ready . . . Fire . . . Aim

IT WAS a tongue twister of a name: the Mutual Medical Aid and Accident Insurance Company, of Chattanooga, Tennessee. Unhappier still was the fact that the company's five officers knew little and cared less about insurance when they opened for business on May 24, 1887. Nor did they learn quickly.

Two weeks passed before President Robert F. Craig, a lawyer whose political ambitions would bring him to grief, thought it wise to gather a few medical statistics of the sort ordinarily used to figure premiums and benefits. None of his colleagues saw any harm in the idea, and so Vice President Reuben H. Hunt took time off from his architectural practice to find out what the town's doctors knew about the frequency of diseases and accidents. Meanwhile, the company kept on writing policies.

To their credit, Craig and the others had spotted an opportunity that, in the right hands, would make several men rich beyond their wildest dreams. It originated in a fact of geology. An underground island of black diamond stretches from Pittsburgh in the north to Birmingham in the south. Its southern expanse remained a blank spot on the map until the 1870s, when mineral hunters, mostly ex-Union officers in the pay of northern financiers, probed its depths. What they found were the nation's richest stores of bituminous

3

coal, alongside quantities of iron ore, timber and water such as could be found in combination nowhere else east of the Mississippi.

The discovery touched off a coal rush, spearheaded by northern industrialists who sent an army of agents south to buy up land and mineral rights. They came by the thousands to East Tennessee, setting up head-quarters in Chattanooga and Knoxville and transform-ing those sleepy towns into booming centers for devel-opment of the surrounding mineral wealth. "Go ring your bell and fire your gun, shout glory, for the 'Boom' has come," proclaimed the Chattanooga *Times* in 1879.

In less than a decade Chattanooga grew from a vil-lage, too poor to buy coal for meetings of its aldermen, into a thriving city known for its smokestacks and rude vigor, a place where the first electric lights went up over streets that wagon wheels churned to mud in a heavy rain. Armed robberies were frequent, fires that gutted whole blocks not uncommon, and lynchings not unknown. But by 1887 Chattanooga's future as an in-dustrial power looked bright, dazzlingly bright to local observers. That May the city's Roane Iron Company produced the first rails of Bessemer steel ever made below the Mason-Dixon Line. Two months earlier, while a land boom sent property values soaring, a group of local developers announced the formation of what was immediately hailed in the local press as the "most gigantic company yet in the South," an enter-prise with a name as long as its agenda: the Chatta-nooga Land, Coal, Iron and Railway Company. Plans called for a capitalization of $12 million, but neglected to specify how that kind of money would be raised in a city whose total banking capital was $2 million. No matter. Civic boosters led by Adolf S. Ochs, the 29-year-old publisher of the *Times,* were confidently predicting that Chattanooga was destined to become the "Pittsburgh of the South." Few citizens doubted it.

In the feverish excitement of the times, a company like the Mutual Medical Aid and Accident Insurance Company could dare to be great.

What the company's founders proposed doing was to insure the uninsurables, the workers at the bottom of the industrial pyramid who performed some of the most dangerous work in America. Nearby sawmills employed 3,200 of them, and thousands more worked the mines, blast furnaces, coke ovens, and rolling mills that had sprung up in and around Chattanooga. They were untouchable risks in the estimation of the old-line insurance companies in Hartford and New York. Accidents happened routinely, leaving men crippled or dead, their families without means of subsistence. A man who could no longer work drew no wages and could expect no relief other than what his fellow workers might collect for him when they passed the hat. The Mutual Medical Aid and Accident Insurance Company offered him a more definite way to make provisions for his family. In return for a monthly premium of 75¢, or half a nickel a day, the company promised to pay an injured worker a sum ranging from $7.50 a week for time lost to $150 for loss of two limbs, or the same amount to his family in case of his death. It was an attractive policy to the common laborer, for whom $150 represented about four months' wages. But a policy was only as good as the company that issued it, and the Mutual Medical Aid had problems.

One problem surfaced when the board met on July 5, in the company's one-room office at 119 East Eighth Street, a nondescript brownstone situated between the Yee Wah Laundry and the Hazard Powder Company. Attendance at these meetings was usually light, since the officers could not often spare time away from their fulltime pursuits. President Robert Craig and his brother John practiced law and politics; Vice President Reuben H. Hunt designed buildings; Secretary A. M. Womble audited the books of the Union Railway; and Richard F. Curd traded real estate in a small way. On this occasion, however, all of them showed up, wearing the worried looks of men about to pay dearly for their mistakes. They were there to liquidate the company's medical-aid business.

It was a painful but necessary step, for according to Hunt's survey of local doctors, medical aid insurance was a losing proposition. A single yellow fever epidemic, such as the one in 1878 that killed 368 in Chattanooga, could wipe out several medical aid insurance companies, and for that reason most life insurance policies excluded travel south of Virginia and Kentucky during the yellow fever season of June 1 to November 1. Seeing disaster ahead, the officers threw operations into reverse, buying back at considerable cost their mistakes, some 100 medical-aid policies. Henceforth, the officers resolved and duly recorded in their minute book, the company would sell only accident insurance, to "persons of sound mind and bodily health, of temperate and moral habits between the ages of 16 and 55 years."

Soon after the misadventure in medical aid, most of the officers discovered pressing obligations that forced their resignations from the company. First to go was John Craig, followed by Richard Curd, who bowed out when the board levied a $150 assessment to make the books balance. Deficits were common, and the officers, as members of a mutual assessment company, were required to chip in the difference or fold. Next to go was President Robert Craig, a glib talker by all accounts, who soon got himself elected county trustee. While in office he suffered attacks of paranoia, and during one of them, he shot and killed the company's secretary, A. M. Womble. Although acquitted, Craig never recovered from the incident and was last seen running a tramp steamer in Cuba.

To replace Craig as president, the board chose John W. Thornton, an executive of the Lookout Iron Company. Other new additions included J. S. Hunnicutt, a bookkeeper at the Third National Bank; M. A. Timothy, whose family owned dry goods stores in Chattanooga and Nashville; J. S. O'Neale, cashier of the Chattanooga National Bank, who married a sister of William Gibbs McAdoo and went east with McAdoo to build the Hudson River Tunnel connecting Manhattan with New Jersey; and Napoleon Loder, a clever young businessman who would make his fortune by inventing and selling something he called "frictionless metal."

Along with the new directors came a new name for the company, one reflecting the board's intention to substitute life insurance for the failed medical aid line. So it was that on December 23, 1887, the directors incorporated the Provident Life and Accident Insurance Company.

Although the plan to sell life insurance fell through, the name stuck. Little else did. President Thornton resigned in March of 1888, and for the next 21 months affairs apparently were so muddled that no one saw the point in keeping minutes. When the practice resumed, late in 1889, the secretary recorded that during the interim four of the nine directors had resigned, three new ones had joined the board, chaired now by Hunt, and the company had moved its office to Room 9 of the Montague Block.

Adding to Provident's troubles was the steady erosion of its economic base. Chattanooga's prospects of becoming the industrial capital of the South, a place where an accident insurance company would never want for business, evaporated when local iron ores proved unsuitable for steel-making. As a consequence, the city's steel industry transferred most of its operations to Birmingham, which grew into the "Pittsburgh of the South," while Chattanooga developed at a slower pace. Development soon came to a standstill, however, as a financial panic swept the nation. Businesses defaulted right and left, and local bank deposits fell from $4.5 million to $1.5 million. Recovery was slow in coming; before the worst was over, seven of Chattanooga's banks collapsed. The panic also deprived Chattanooga of several ardent civic boosters. Two of them, Adolf S. Ochs and William Gibbs McAdoo, suffered financial reversals and repaired to New York, where both went on to fame and fortune—Ochs as publisher of the New York *Times,* and McAdoo as son-in-law of President Woodrow Wilson and a Democratic presidential hopeful who narrowly missed nomination.

By the spring of 1892, Provident had a dismal record to show for its first five years of business. Fifteen directors had come and gone. Of the original incorporators only Hunt remained. The company had moved five times, from one tiny office to another, often struggling to pay a $15-a-month rent. It had exactly 850 accident policies on the books, not nearly enough to bring into play the laws of probability that keep insurance companies profitable. In theory, the company collected $7,800 in premiums annually. In practice, the amount was usually closer to $5,000, which, coincidentally, was also the amount of capital that the present officers had invested. The return on investment being what it was, the officers showed no reluctance to share ownership with others. In fact, they considered it a stroke of luck when two Scotsmen by the names of Thomas Maclellan and John McMaster came along and offered to pay $1,000 for half interest in Provident.

2

A Second Beginning

LIKE PROVIDENT ITSELF, Thomas Maclellan and John McMaster had fallen on hard times. They saw in the troubled insurance company a chance, not a great chance but perhaps their last, to make a fresh start. Both 54 years old, they were starting over at a time when most men their age were nodding by the fire.

Maclellan, a soft-spoken man with opaque brown eyes and the slight burr of the Scottish Highlands in his voice, had been born the son of a shoemaker in the village of Castle Douglas. It was the sort of place where a shoemaker's son grew up to become a shoemaker himself. Thomas took work as a bank clerk, instead. At 25, he wrote a prize-winning essay on banking that won him appointment as manager of the British Bank of North America, in St. John, New Brunswick. On Christmas Day of 1862 he sailed for the New World, never to return to the Old. Twenty-five years later he was president and second largest stockholder of the St. John's Maritime Bank and one of the town's leading citizens. Then he made a miscalculation, the consequences of which would have broken the spirit of a lesser man.

The miscalculation involved "debtor's leverage," a situation arising when a borrower owes enough to break the bank if he defaults and thus is in a position

to dictate terms to the bank. For years the Maritime
had turned a respectable profit by financing companies
engaged in commercial shipping. But when that industry declined in the mid-1880s, Maritime was left holding several non-producing loans made to two companies. In an effort to save these loans, the bank lent
the two companies increasingly large sums over a period of months, always accepting as collateral the optimistic forecasts of the companies' executives. Before
long, Maritime was at the mercy of its debtors. On the
morning of March 7, 1887, Maclellan and the other
officers waited for a large deposit promised by one of
the shipping executives; without it the bank could not
open its doors. The deposit never came, and the Maritime collapsed.

"It is a miserable story," Maclellan confessed with
quiet dignity to the shareholders assembled a month
later to liquidate Maritime. "It costs me my good name
in this community where I have lived for a quarter
of a century, and which I had expected would be my
permanent home. It has blotted out my home and the
home of those who bear my name. It has caused grief
and loss to my friends, and it has spread suffering
among those who had a right to expect from me better
things. I did not intentionally bring this calamity to
others. I expected the promises made by customers
would be performed, and it may, perhaps, be accepted
as some evidence I did so think, however infatuated
the belief may appear, that I gave no one any hint of
the possible collapse, nor did I in any way protect myself, my relatives, my partner or my friends."

No one who knew Maclellan could doubt that his
conduct had been principled, even if his trust had been
misplaced. "He was brought up on oatmeal and cate-
chism," remarked one friend, by way of explaining

Maclellan's plain manner and fierce integrity. Indeed, he was a devout Covenanter who followed to the letter the teachings of that zealous Presbyterian sect, described by one authority this way: "What the Puritan was to England and the Huguenot was to France, the Covenanter was to Scotland." Maclellan, the rigidly upright Covenanter, promised to repay all who felt that by any act of his they had lost money in the Maritime debacle. To find a position where he could earn the money, along with enough to support his family and himself, and in so doing regain the good name that had always been his, he would have to re-establish himself in business.

Eating the crust of humility, Maclellan took to the road, leaving his wife and children in St. John while he searched for a position, first in New York, then in Philadelphia. There he joined up with his friend John McMaster, a fellow Scotsman and Covenanter whose import firm in Hamilton, Ontario was going down with all hands. The two were a study in contrast, McMaster as gregarious and passionately intense as Maclellan was reserved and cooly calculating. McMaster, remembering a Canadian who had gone to Shanghai with $50 and returned 12 years later with $250,000, suggested that the pair head for China. Maclellan was not persuaded. He did, however, drift westward with McMaster, stopping in towns in Pennsylvania, Ohio, Missouri, Colorado and Kansas. In letters home, Maclellan often poked fun at his friend's talent for self-promotion. "If I could blow my horn as well as Mr. McMaster can, I would be more likely to succeed. He is quite a Boanerges," grumbled Maclellan, alluding to the Biblical "sons of thunder," so called for their rhetorical fireworks. When McMaster rhapsodized about how a concoction of his, an elixir he

named Kanela, would make them both rich, Maclellan
wrote: "He is so puffed up with his Kanela that he
thinks there is nothing like it. He blows about it—
'It never fails, was never known to fail, great is Kanela.'
I have always smiled and not gone into ecstasies
over it."

The two parted company amicably when Maclellan,
wearying of the nomadic life, decided to settle in
Topeka, Kansas. But before he could send for his family, he received word from St. John that his daughter,
Bessie, had died suddenly. In this calamity Maclellan
saw the inexorable hand of Providence shaping all
things for the best. To his son Robert he wrote:

"The Lord has been speaking loudly and I hope we
will heed His voice. Bessie was only lent to us, and
her Owner had the right to take her back when He
saw best. I agreed to this when, for instance at her
baptism, I gave her back to God, and now I have not
a word to say against her removal. The Lord said 'take
this child and nurse her for Me and I will give thee
thy wages.' I am ashamed to think of the wages if they
be according to what I did, but full of joy that Jesus
Christ, our Prophet, trained her Himself, and that there
is some evidence that she has gone to be with Him.
And I hope He has been teaching you also and that
the Holy Spirit has been graciously dealing with your
soul, leading you to assent to what we did for you at
your baptism, and to, of your own choice, take God
as your portion—willing to live or die as He sees best
and if not to die then to live a life of faith and love
and zealous service as one who is not his own, but be-
longing to the Lord. . . ."

A few months later Maclellan's family joined him
in Topeka, and for nearly two years the ex-bank president held a succession of lowly jobs: selling encyclope-

dias, clerking in the business office of a local newspaper, and bookkeeping for the Santa Fe Railroad at a salary of $50 a month.

A thousand or so miles away, in Chattanooga, John McMaster was writing Maclellan enthusiastic letters about the opportunities available in the "New South." Urging that they join forces again, McMaster wrote, "I have a conviction that we would be a strong team." Maclellan, dogged by hard luck in Topeka, thought Chattanooga worth a look. With luck or, as he preferred to express it, with "God's Providence . . . opening the way," he might yet re-establish himself in business. Exactly what he would find in Chattanooga, he did not know. But the Presbyterian deacon set off with the firm belief that he would be "led and held by God in His right hand, . . . [in] Chattanooga, as well as anywhere else."

What he found on arriving, in March of 1892, was not altogether to his liking. "There are some fine buildings, and along the river's edge lots of big mills and factories. But it is a slouchy place, behind the age. It is suffering from depressed times, but yet there appear to be wonderfully few houses to rent. The climate is more like Scotland than Kansas, at least in winter, and on the whole not as healthy perhaps as Kansas," he reported to Helen, his wife, with his usual keen eye for detail. His reservations increased as he fell into the familiar role of disappointed job seeker. The Third National Bank turned him down for a position as bookkeeper. He wrote employment-wanted ads that went unanswered. Time weighed heavily: "Nothing today from anyone. Another day gone." He smiled politely when McMaster talked of the Kanela elixir. After three weeks of searching for work and meeting with rejection, he bought a half-fare rail ticket, packed his bag, and on March 30 informed Helen, "I am preparing to leave tonight at 7:00."

Then luck—or Providence—intervened in the form of an offer from Alexander Glover, a friend of McMaster's. Glover's real estate firm needed a decent set of books. Would Maclellan stay long enough to set up a double-entry system? Agreeing to stay, Maclellan wrote Helen: "It was what I was put to when I went to St. John. [But] if I give [Glover] satisfaction in opening up his books, I will have satisfaction and no doubt he will give me something, probably as much as I had in Topeka. If I get the same I will be able to send you half of it."

McMaster, while making a living by penning advertisements for Angier's Dry Goods, had kept a sharp eye out for some business in which he and Maclellan could go partners. He turned up two possibilities the week after Maclellan began work. Both required an investment of $1,000. One was the Pure Gold Manufacturing Company, which, said its organizers, would soon be producing ink, glue, soap, coat hangers and railway ties. The other was Provident. According to Reuben Hunt, the little insurance company was a diamond in the rough, but he had "no time to attend to it." Maclellan filled notebooks with calculations of income-to-profit ratios. He and McMaster interviewed one of the company's traveling agents and found in him an admirable spirit of enlightened self-interest: an "excellent man [who] expects to do well for himself and this means, of course, doing well for the company." The more they looked at Pure Gold the better they liked Provident. On April 27, Maclellan wired Helen, "Closed with insurance company. Seek transportation now. Leave when agreeable."

The two Scotsmen were under no illusions about

what they had purchased. Maclellan, in fact, contemplated taking an extra job to supplement the paltry salary he would draw from Provident. But they both believed in the plan to sell accident insurance, even though it had been carried out in accidental fashion for five years. To put matters aright, they intended to sell sound policies in numbers sufficiently large to offset the high risks being insured. "We were satisfied that our plan was a winner," McMaster afterward explained. "It needed only expansion as the way to success."

There was, however, a catch. Provident could expand only as fast as public confidence in insurance grew. And on the scale of popular opinion, the insurance business ranked somewhere between the white-slave trade and yellow journalism. Unsound insurance companies had sprung up, in the words of one historian, "like gnats on a summer's evening and disappeared as quickly." Because many of these companies had promised more than they ever delivered, most people regarded the entire industry with deep suspicion. Reflecting the general mistrust, public buildings often displayed signs barring "peddlers, solicitors and insurance agents." Given the prevailing mood, Maclellan and McMaster decided that making friends with a hostile public was essential, even at the cost of immediate profits. They accordingly committed the company to "pay all just claims promptly," which was then regarded in some quarters as an extravagant practice. Nearly every claim was to be adjusted and paid the same week received and, in fact, some unfair claims were paid to win a reputation for "square dealing."

McMaster, a balding, bewhiskered man with pluck and a knack for winning friends, assumed the duties of general manager. It was his job to "do the rustling around, get into labor union meetings and spout, come into contact with working men, employ agents, handle men and work up a business." This meant going down into the mines, where McMaster had to watch not only for prospects but also for cave-ins, rockfalls and explosions. The life of a miner was hard, dangerous and exhausting. He was paid not by the hour but by the carload of coal he gouged out of the earth—about 75¢ for each load of 2.5 tons. Under the circumstances, he was naturally reluctant to lay down his pick and listen to talk about insurance. For that reason, another agent went along to relieve a miner while McMaster explained to him about the half-nickel-a-day policy. There were other obstacles as well. Sometimes mine owners took a dim view of insurance agents, suspecting them of planting fancy ideas into the heads of working men. On at least one occasion, McMaster was drummed off a property by gun-slinging guards. Other times, the miners themselves proved difficult. In Ducktown, Tennessee, where the corrosive fumes of the Tennessee Copper Company's smelting pits were turning the landscape into a 23,000-acre wasteland, McMaster solicited 107 miners before selling a policy.

The view from the home office was none too cheery, either. Maclellan took charge of the office, which was located at the northwest corner of Seventh and Market, in the Richardson Building. There he strained to put the company on a sound financial footing. As secretary, he monitored the receipt of premiums, collected monthly by "payorder" arrangement. This meant that the paymaster who doled out a policyholder's wages also deducted from them the 75¢ premium and, after taking a commission of ten percent, sent the balance to Provident. But even when all the paymasters remitted on time, which was the exception rather than the rule, expenses and claims tended to exceed income. Such was the case in January of 1893. With expenses of $460.90 and a bank balance of $120, the company was forced to borrow $325 to meet its obligations. It must have been tempting to stall for time by delaying claim payments. Instead, Maclellan and McMaster chose to go without their salaries and continue to pay "every just claim promptly." As McMaster later put it, "Sink or swim our determination was to do a square business, believing that if the plan was right, honesty and grit would be a sure winner."

Whether there was more to it than honesty and grit, the fact remains that Provident began to show signs of life in April 1893. McMaster had managed to more than double the number of policyholders, from 850 to 1750, and in doing so had signed up the company's first railroadmen, employees of the Chattanooga Southern. Maclellan's books registered a profit of $1,031. Taking note of the company's "upward course," the Chattanooga *News* called Provident a "strong Institution . . . a boon to working men." The *News* went on to point out that "the cost to the men is only 75¢ per month and is never felt by them. Every just claim against the company has been paid with a promptness seldom equalled by insurance men." Typical of the claimants was one Rufus Stair, of Westbourne, Tennessee, who collected $6.40 after a mine mule kicked him in the face.

Although continuing to concentrate activities in Chattanooga and East Tennessee, the company gradually established toeholds in West Virginia, Alabama, Georgia and Virginia. In 1894 premiums began to trickle in from out-of-state concerns, such as the Bertha Zinc Works, of Pulaski, Virginia; the Elkhorn Coal and Coke Company, of May Bury, West Virginia; and the Dayton Coal and Iron Company, of Bronco, Georgia.

Workers at the mammoth Sloss Iron and Steel Company, in Birmingham, joined the growing list of customers in 1895.

That same year Maclellan and McMaster bought out all the other owners of Provident. McMaster took over as president, and Maclellan retained the posts of secretary and treasurer. Even though Maclellan's financial investment in the company now surpassed that of his friend, the two continued as they had begun, equal partners. "We agree," read the contract they signed, "that our interest be identical and that we share and share alike in future profits and losses." Further, they bound themselves to plow profits back into the company, agreeing to "draw on our accounts only an equal moderate amount for living for the present."

*   *   *   *   *

At the tail end of the 19th century, the chief concern in the minds of Maclellan and McMaster was to rid Provident of the stigma attached to its line of business. Fly-by-night operators had poisoned the well for the accident insurance industry as a whole. So numerous were the defaults that, according to the *National Insurance Leader*, the "business shores of the South were whitened with the bones of insurance companies that had foundered on the shoals of inexperience and mismanagement." As a pioneering company in a new and still suspect field, Provident strived to throw off the assumption of guilt by association. The company's advertisements continually emphasized corporate principles rather than products. Slogans such as "No Red Tape," and "The Old Reliable Provident" appeared like trademarks on letterheads and brochures. In 1899 the company distributed a bookmark-size advertisement that took the tone of an aggressive brief for the defense:

OUR PLAN COVERS

Every form of accidental injury, and is good anywhere, except for violation of the law of the land or occurring in a saloon.

The policy is a plain, liberal contract with no obscure conditions to vitiate it . . .

Dozens of companies have copied our plan, bloomed out for a short time, *then died. We still live for others to imitate.* . . .

The managers of the Provident Life and Accident Insurance Company are men of integrity. . . .

NOT AN UNPAID CLAIM!

The advertisement then offered the testimony of supporting witnesses. One was policyholder R. R. Price, of Ducktown, who wrote: "I was pleased to receive your check for $90.00 yesterday. I got $90.00 in gold for it five minutes afterwards. So I can't say too much for the old Provident, and I would advise every workingman to insure in your company." Another was J. E. Johnson, manager of the Longdale Iron Company, who wrote: "It gives us pleasure to say that for a year past some of our men have been insuring with your company against accidents. So far it has given great satisfaction. The men who have been injured have been promptly paid the amounts due them, while to a certain extent it has been a protection against their indebtedness to us."

Nonetheless, the jury of public opinion remained deadlocked on the issue. For decades to come Provident entered more evidence into the record, including long lists of claims paid each month, with names, amounts, and sometimes even the addresses of claimants, should skeptics wish to verify the information.

To their agents in the field, Maclellan and McMaster preached ethics as well as salesmanship, square-dealing as well as deal-closing. "In soliciting, be very careful to always state the truth and nothing but the truth," admonished Provident's handbook for agents. "The insurance we offer is of such merit that there is no need for misrepresentation. The plain, unvarnished facts will always make our work popular." In practice, though, some agents embellished freely on the facts. One of these agents was an ex-coal miner named James (Buddy) Stokes, who stuttered badly. He would go down into a mine and, as the miners gathered around, pick out one of them and, stammering as if his memory were too vivid for the human tongue to express, tell his audience that he had had a terrible dream about the man. He had dreamt that a piece of slate fell on the man and cut off his leg and that his wife and children were starving because the man had no accident insurance. He must have been a spell-binding performer, for Buddy Stokes was consistently among the company's top salesmen.

* * * * *

The beginning of the new century marked the end of a management era for Provident. McMaster and Maclellan had always been poles apart in temperament. McMaster was all fire and air, Maclellan earth and water. They had, nonetheless, complemented each other as partners in a company that needed both a doer out in the field and a thinker back in the office. But as they grew older they also grew apart. Their differences mounted until, in 1900, the two Scotsmen ended their partnership. Earlier they had agreed that in case of a rift the company would go to the one of them making the higher bid. The high bidder was Maclellan, who assumed the presidency while McMaster departed for West Virginia to start an insurance company of his own.

A few days before leaving, McMaster wrote a letter in which he laid bare his wounded feelings. Dispensing with the usual salutation of "Dear Friend," or "Dear Brother," he wrote:

> Dear Mr. Maclellan: I want to say that I desire your forgiveness for any word of mine that in any way may have annoyed or grieved you in the past relationship. At the same time I desire to forgive you for many things that have given me annoyance. Little things it is true, such as lack of openness, frankness, and candour, all very small compared to my offenses against you. For which I desire forgiveness even as I seek to forgive. I am sincerely yours, John McMaster.

McMaster's exit left Provident without a strong hand to guide sales. Maclellan, now 64, his sight growing dim in one eye, felt uneasy as he shouldered the added responsibilities of recruiting and handling agents. Carrying on alone seemed to him an ordeal. On the day before it began, he recorded in his prayer book a fervent plea to God to give him "faith, love, repentance, more desire to glorify Thee," among other spiritual blessings. "And now," he continued, "about the business and worldly things. . . . Raise up friends, keep down opposition, and let the business prosper and give us a living in peace and without great strain to my mind and body. Without Thy blessing it will be a disaster. Gracious Lord, enable me to carry it on successfully, or raise up some who will take it over, or join me, or whatever will be best for Thy Glory and my good."

On the temporal plane, it was to his children that Maclellan turned for aid. Daughter Dora lightened the load in 1901 by taking over the office of secretary. Five years later she yielded the post to her brother Robert J., 31, who also signed on as treasurer. A gentlemanly, formal man, slightly on guard against vague dangers, Robert, like his father, was quiet and conscientious and kept his own counsel. In 1892 he had served as Provident's office boy, a job that, as he remembered it, consisted mainly of pasting huge gilt seals on policies, without which decoration the "policyholder did not think he was getting full value." Then he had left the company for a series of administrative jobs in local government and banking. On Robert's return, Provident became a father-son operation, held together as much by ties of blood as by ties of business.

The team of father and son added two lines to Provident's coverage. First was sickness insurance, which at a monthly premium of 75¢ provided an indemnity of $4.50 a week for 15 weeks. The other was industrial insurance, also known as debit insurance, which consisted of policies sold door-to-door to small wage earners—maids, salesclerks, housewives—who paid their premiums when the insurance man came round each week to collect. But these and other efforts to expand produced mixed results, primarily because the sales force lacked direction. This was particularly true of debit insurance, for at its head was a vice president who had the habit of losing touch with the home office for weeks on end, usually at times when he had neglected to remit money due the company. Consequently, earnings fluctuated unpredictably. Salaries were set not at the beginning of the year but at the end, and sometimes not even then. In January of 1906 the minutes noted that "the fixing of the president's salary for the past year was held over for future action, the earnings of the company not justifying payment."

At the same time, events beyond Maclellan's control were rapidly overtaking Provident. In 1905 the Armstrong Committee, impanelled by the New York Legislature and chaired by Charles Evans Hughes, launched a sweeping investigation of the state's insurance industry. The hearings generated considerable public interest, particularly when they uncovered a witch's brew of corporate misconduct, including executive salaries approaching $100,000 a year, flagrant disregard of policyholders' rights and insufficient reserves to meet claims. Responding to the ensuing public outcry, state legislatures enacted reforms which, among other provisions, required insurance companies to post larger reserves, a kind of bond in case a company defaulted on its policyholders. When Alabama and West Virginia raised their reserve requirements in 1909, capital-strapped Provident had no choice but to withdraw from those two states. It was left with three states and the imminent likelihood of more shrinkage in its territory.

As a further result of the Armstrong hearings, insurance companies flocked to the Midwest and South, where regulatory laws, though stiffened, made those newly adopted in the Northeast look unduly severe. Thus, Provident faced the twin threats of shrinking territory and rising competition, neither of which it was financially prepared to meet. The way Maclellan figured it, he had three choices in 1909. He could try to "sell out." That failing, he could "quit." Or else he could raise money, find new partners and reorganize "on a capitalized basis." For his own part, he confessed a longing to be done with the "strife and annoyances in a business with unscrupulous opponents and agents." But it was no longer that simple. Now that

Robert was a part of the company, Provident was a branch of the Maclellan family. In the fall of 1909 Thomas Maclellan reached a decision. If he could raise $150,000 in working capital and still hold on to his family's controlling interest in Provident, then he would soldier on

3

"Energy and Brains . . .
Much in Demand"

ALEXANDER WILDS CHAMBLISS, born in 1864, while his father was serving as a Baptist chaplain in Lee's Army, moved back and forth between boardrooms, courtrooms and smoke-filled back rooms as effortlessly as a gifted linguist switches from High German to Low Dutch in mid-thought. As a politician, he ran for office four times and was four times elected. As a jurist, he rose to become Chief Justice of the Tennessee Supreme Court. When Adolf S. Ochs left Chattanooga to buy the New York *Times,* attorney Chambliss went along to handle the legal details. Equally adept as a financier, he amassed land, securities and companies in such quantities that his son later quipped, "I've spent most of my life inheriting things."

If anybody in Chattanooga could put together the deal that Thomas Maclellan had in mind, that person was Chambliss. Since 1895 he had acted as Provident's lawyer, and in 1909, at Maclellan's urging, he undertook to reorganize the company. The plan was to merge the old mutual business into a new stock company having sufficient capital to expand. All agreed that nothing less than $150,000 would do. Of that amount, $100,000 was to be common stock and $50,000 preferred—a formula arrived at when it became apparent that the Maclellans and those they wished to have as partners could raise only $100,000. Thus the preferred shares, being non-voting and subject to retirement at the end of eight years, served the purpose of raising the additional capital without diluting ownership. But there was the matter of finding buyers for the preferred stock. In this, the resourceful Chambliss proved his worth as an investment broker.

Some fairly deep pockets of wealth had formed in Chattanooga since the 1880s, and sitting atop one of the deeper of them was Mrs. Edward Gould Richmond, a widow and transplanted Ohioan whose husband had inherited $10 million, migrated south and started one of Chattanooga's first textile mills. Besides holding title to large chunks of downtown Chattanooga, including the future site of the American National Bank and Trust Company, Mrs. Richmond numbered among her properties the Richmond Spinning Mill, the Richmond Cotton Oil Company and the Richmond Hosiery Mill. With money to invest but no inclination to sit on boards or otherwise involve herself in business affairs, she seemed ideally to answer Provident's need for a silent investor. At least Chambliss thought so, and he should have known, since he was her lawyer as well as a stockholder in the Richmond Spinning Mill. Business relationships in Chattanooga were beginning to resemble an intricate family tree, a tapestry of interlocking directorships binding together bankers, manufacturers and merchants. Chambliss intended to weave Provident into this rich fabric. In the early winter of 1909 he called on Mrs. Richmond, explained the proposition, told her that he planned to invest $10,000 himself, and left with her pledge to take the entire issue of preferred stock. In one stroke, and with "less difficulty" than Maclellan had "feared," the problem of capital was solved.

When it came to divvying up the 1,000 shares of common stock, Thomas and Robert J. Maclellan acquired 501 shares, and Chambliss took 100, together with a vice-presidency in the company. The remaining 399 shares were earmarked as a goodwill offering, for, as Maclellan explained, the shares went to "mine owners to keep them from giving any other company the business at their mines." That the directors distributed some 40 percent of Provident's voting stock in this way is a measure of the importance they placed on winning the goodwill of mine owners and other employers. Without an employer's consent, Provident's agents could not have come within shouting distance of workers, since the employer owned not only the mine or mill but also the houses and the very town in which workers lived. And even though it was the worker who would pay the entire cost of insurance, the employer sometimes objected to insurance coverage for fear that a disability payment would deprive an injured worker of the incentive to return to the job promptly upon recovery. Thus, in a letter dated August 15, 1914, did the president of Roden Coal Company, of Marvel, Alabama, write Maclellan expressing pleasant surprise that Roden Coal had not "found a case where [Provident's insurance] tended to keep a miner from work as soon as he was able."

When asking permission to solicit workers, the Provident agent avoided appeals to an employer's altruistic impulses. This was just as well, considering that most employers conceived of workers' insurance in terms similar to those expressed in a letter of July 31, 1911, by one W. H. Heffelfinger, general manager of the Tellico River Lumber Company: ". . . the man who holds a Provident policy is not likely to annoy the Company in case of sickness or injury." Traditionally, southern management had granted laborers small advances to tide them over spells of disability. But lately this practice had fallen into disfavor, particularly with the management of large companies which, like the Tellico River Lumber Company, were controlled by absentee owners in the Northeast. By permitting the introduction of insurance, argued the Provident agent, management could spare itself the annoyance of providing for injured workers; Provident would, in effect, assume the responsibility for industrial welfare. It was an effective selling point. And to make it even more attractive, Provident offered financial inducements. A company was allowed to keep ten percent of the premiums collected by its paymaster, who was entitled to receive all claim payments and, before distributing them, deduct any amounts an injured worker might owe the company store. As a further inducement, Provident's directors offered their company's stock, knowing that an employer who received dividends was likely to collect premiums diligently and speak well of workers' insurance.

The reorganization became official on January 31, 1910, when Tennessee's Secretary of State issued a corporate charter to the Provident Life and Accident Insurance Company of Chattanooga. As if marking a transition to bigger things, the usual handwritten accounts of board meetings gave way to neatly typed minutes. In addition to the Maclellans and Chambliss, the board now consisted of James B. F. Lowry, cashier of the Citizens National Bank; and Morgan Llewellyn, father-in-law of Robert J. Maclellan. A portly Welshman who tipped the scales at 300 pounds, Llewellyn is best remembered for his part in building the Hedges, Walsh and Weidner Boiler Company into what would become, as a subsidiary of Combustion Engineering, one of

Chattanooga's leading manufacturers. With Chambliss, Llewellyn and Lowry on the board, Provident began gradually to break out of the pattern of two-man management that had characterized the company since 1895.

The trend toward a more diverse style of management received further impetus as the Maclellans hired managers to fill the organizational void that had long existed in the middle range between the boardroom and the field. Shrewd judges of men, the Maclellans excelled as talent scouts. In a year's time father and son recruited three able and eager young men destined to leave lasting imprints on the company. James Washington Kirksey, the first to arrive, was born in the backwoods of Sand Mountain, Georgia, in 1882. As a young man whose aspirations exceeded his prospects, Kirksey had thrown himself into a harsh regimen of study and self-improvement. Working in the fields by day and studying accounting by night, he eventually won a position as paymaster at the Southern Iron and Steel Company, where his duties included handling the payorder agreement between Southern's workers and Provident. This brought him in contact with R. J. Maclellan who, impressed with Kirksey's efficiency as well as his burning ambition, hired him away from Southern. From then on Kirksey lived and breathed Provident, a point that his daughter once underlined when she confessed herself at a loss to "separate my father from his work." His specialty was the payorder business, to which he applied himself with a determination akin to fanaticism. As one observer later recalled, it was not unusual for Kirksey to "get up at six o'clock, catch a train and ride it up to LaFollette, get off, then get on a mule and ride it to a mine, and go down into the mine and solicit two shifts of miners." By 1914 he headed the Payorder Department and in 1916 was named a director.

Not long after Kirksey joined the company, Thomas Maclellan received a letter from another aspiring young man interested in going to work for Provident. Maclellan wrote back, "We will be glad to see you, to talk over your coming to help us make the Provident a success. Energy and brains are much in demand these days." The young man, a 23-year-old paymaster at the Wind Rock Coal Company, was a Kentuckian of sturdy German stock by the name of William Carl Cartinhour. Although Maclellan could not have known it at the time, Cartinhour would be for Provident a one-man reservoir of energy and ideas. Steely-eyed and square-jawed, Cartinhour possessed a capacious memory and an intellect that went straight to the heart of problems. Before turning 30, he would be second in command at Provident.

Rounding out the trio of newcomers was Leslie Nabors Webb, 24, hale, hearty and invincibly charming. When he applied for a job, Thomas and R. J. Maclellan let him know that the company was "small and money was hard to come by," but if he were really willing to work and forget about office hours, they would give him a try. Whatever doubts they might have entertained about Webb were speedily resolved in his favor. By 1916 he headed the Claims Department, and his diplomatic skills made him much in demand as a wooer of difficult clients and a mediator of internal disputes. When an agent hit the skids, it was Webb who cleaned up the mess. Typical of these personnel problems was the case of a general agent, Mr. M, whose distraught wife wrote Webb, explaining that Mr. M had taken to drinking up premiums faster than they could be collected. "He has gone on a drinking spree and is spending the money that is coming in," she wrote. "No one here has the authority or ability to stop it. He is being held in a disreputable hotel of which the matron has the reputation of extracting a drinking man's last dollar. He gives checks which none of us can prevent being cashed, and we all know that the business is not in financial status to stand the tremendous drain. I am wondering if you could come here at once and take possession of the accounts so that none of these drinking checks can be paid." Webb did exactly that, and over the next six months negotiated the sale of the faltering agency, a transaction that worked to the mutual benefit of Provident and Mr. M.

The infusion of talent and capital soon made itself felt. In 1911 Provident doubled its territory by entering North Carolina, Georgia and Alabama; applications were made for licenses in the District of Columbia and Florida as well. Another indicator of performance, premium income, jumped from $120,000 in 1909 to $308,000 in 1911. Encouraged by the upward trend, the directors decided that Provident had outgrown its one-room office, now located in the Temple Court Building at the southeast corner of Seventh and Cherry. In October the employees packed up their desks and ledgers and carted them two blocks away to new quarters, the seventh floor of the swank James Building. Owned by railroad tycoon Charles Edward James, this highrise structure, the first of its kind in Chattanooga, sported 1,000 windows and 700 doors. A year later the company was on the move again, this time to the James Building Annex. In one of those small ironies of history, this tiny but elegant building, with the purity of line and ornamental detail of a Greek temple, had been designed by the man who 20 years earlier had held Provident's highest office, Reuben Harrison Hunt.

Any resemblance between the new home office and a Greek temple vanished as soon as one walked inside. There, amid a jumble of roll-top desks heaped high with paperwork, men in starched collar stocks and bowties bent over ledgers, dipping pens into inkwells and making entries. The sound of scratching pens and rustling papers was punctuated by the staccato clatter of typewriters. Poised over the typewriters were the advance guard of what would become a legion of bustled and bodiced secretaries. Prim, slim and demure, they wore high-button shoes, long skirts that skimmed the floor, shirtwaists fastened modestly under the chin, and high-piled hair-dos. Many, like Miss Frances B. Amos, who would soon head a clerical department, preferred to retain their maiden status all their days, wanting no other family than Provident. There were, however, moments when ladylike decorum was thrown to the winds. John Neligan, a claims adjuster with a lively and endearing sense of the ridiculous, once walked into the office to find the entire staff, ladies included, crouched down on their hands and knees, searching frantically underneath desks. The source of the commotion was rotund Morgan Llewellyn who, while seated at his desk, had sneezed so violently that his false teeth flew out of his mouth and disappeared. The employees were especially anxious to find Llewellyn's teeth, for he was not only Robert Maclellan's father-in-law but also the company's treasurer.

Accompanying the move to more spacious quarters was the arrival of the first professional staff member. Since 1892 Provident had depended on what Maclellan called "energy and brains," rather than on specialized knowledge. No medical officer tracked the shifting patterns of morbidity and mortality. No actuary or statistician applied higher mathematics to the calculation of premiums. "We made up the rates and hoped they were good," said Maclellan years later. That began to change in 1913 when the board hired as medical officer Dr. H. L. Fancher, a graduate of the University of the South Medical School and former chief surgeon at the Campbell Coal and Coke Company. Even so, management retained Dr. Fancher on a part-time basis only, having judged a full-time medical officer to be a luxury beyond their means.

The decision to economize was to be expected in a company where a major client's failure to remit premiums on time could plunge the home office into gloom. As John O. Carter, Jr., bookkeeper and later treasurer, remembered it, "We had some accounts, particularly one in Birmingham—the monthly premium was about $3,000—and if it didn't get in on time, everybody walked around like there had been a death in the family." Waste was a deadly sin, and the Provident *Review,* an internal publication, regularly preached against it. "Stop! Look! Listen! WHO picks up the paper clips you drop on the floor? WHO pays for the pencils you are so careless with? WHO pays for the stationery you waste?" ran one front-page leader.

It would be another five years before the directors hired an actuary and 11 more years before they felt secure enough to retain a full-time medical examiner.

Conserving resources took on added urgency in the fall of 1914, with the outbreak of war in Europe. As the foreign conflict spread, so did domestic fears that the nation would be caught up in it. The mood of uncertainty disrupted financial markets; by 1915 the pinch was felt throughout the Appalachian South as manufacturers cut production and laid off workers. Maclellan reported that policy lapses were running at the rate of 20 percent of insurance in force. To offset the loss, the directors adopted a two-fold strategy. First, they slashed operating expenses, which fell from 13.5 percent of income in 1914 to 10.5 percent in 1915. That figure, Maclellan noted, "compared favorably with the typical 15 percent overhead of the largest insurance companies." Second, they pushed for business in new areas, entering West Virginia, Ohio, Pennsylvania, Texas, Arkansas and Indiana. Fresh sources of income came from Alabama, where Carl Cartinhour negotiated a sizable contract with the Sloss-Sheffield Steel and Iron Company, then followed by purchasing the business of a faltering insurance company. As a result of economies at the home office and aggressive selling in the field, Provident ended the trying year of 1915 with premium income of $439,300, up more than $100,000 over the previous year.

The economy rallied in the winter of 1915 as factories geared up to produce munitions and other war matériel. Within a year the price of coal rose from about 80¢ a ton to as much as $7 a ton for immediate delivery. Mine operators flocked to the Appalachian coal fields. In Pike County, Kentucky, alone, the number of mines increased from 16 in 1916 to 62 in 1920. And men who had never seen $100 in cash in the course of a year came down from the hills in droves to work the black seams at wages upwards of $400 a month. By 1920 there were 11,000 coal miners in Tennessee, 14,000 in Virginia, and 95,000 in West Virginia.

Provident boomed along with the coal industry. At the end of 1916 the company posted a staggering 65.3 percent increase in premium income, an increase equivalent to the entire gains made in the previous five years. With premium income pushing $800,000,

the $1 million mark no longer seemed so remote a
prospect. All agreed that 1916 was the "greatest year
in the company's history."

But pride in achievement was restrained by the loss
of someone who had meant much to Provident. While
vacationing in Massachusetts in August, Thomas Maclellan had gone out for an evening stroll along a shore
road and been struck and fatally injured by a passing
automobile. The sudden and brutal circumstances of
his death moved Alexander Chambliss to write: "While
we knew that we could not hope to have our good friend
among us many years more, this sudden death comes
with a peculiar shock to those of us who knew how
very gentle he was. He seemed to us to deserve to fall
asleep, and through that quiet door to pass out to the
beyond. Unostentatious, so retiring as to be almost
shrinking in disposition, he has never been in the limelight, but pursuing his even, quiet way has built up
one of the biggest and strongest institutions we have."

Of all the tributes paid to his memory, the honorable
Scotsman who had once lost his good name in a business disaster would perhaps have taken greatest satisfaction in the Hamilton County *Herald*'s eulogy: "Mr.
Maclellan was one of the city's most conservative and
substantial businessmen and a man for whom everybody had the most profound respect and who possessed
public confidence as but few men possess it."

*   *   *   *   *

At the board meeting of September 14, 1916, management control of Provident passed officially into the
hands of Robert J. Maclellan, who assumed the presidency. To serve as second-in-command, the board
elected Carl Cartinhour. Under their joint leadership,

the company moved to complete a process of defining the exact nature of its business. This process had begun in 1911 when the company withdrew from the debit insurance market, selling its debits in Chattanooga, Nashville, Memphis, Knoxville and Norfolk to the Peninsular Casualty Company, of Jacksonville. The decision to divest was made partly because the business represented a "large volume but little profit," and partly because the high-pressure sales and collection techniques of debit insurance were not, concluded Thomas Maclellan, in keeping with Provident's policy of "fair dealing."

After the divestiture, two sales departments remained: Payorder, which dealt with groups of employees who paid their premiums through payroll deductions; and Accident, headed by Marshall LeSeuer, which differed from Payorder in so far as it dealt with individuals—usually teachers, doctors, and merchants—who mailed in their premiums. In 1916 a third unit was formed by spinning off Payorder's railroad business into a separate department. Railroading was still a thriving industry. More than 600 different lines criss-crossed the nation, and the stories of John Henry and Casey Jones stirred the popular imagination. Railroading was also dangerous (among brakemen, 63.3 percent of all deaths between 1907 and 1910 occurred as a result of accidents); and it was highly specialized work with a language and culture all its own. Provident's Railroad Department, staffed mainly with former brakemen, engineers and conductors, was designed to meet the large and specialized needs of the industry.

A fourth sales department went into operation on January 1, 1917. On that day, after 30 years of billing

itself as a life insurance company, Provident sold its
first life insurance policy. The client was Robert J. Maclellan. His father had always urged that a Provident
agent should sell his first accident or sickness policy
to himself, and Robert apparently felt that a Provident
president could do no less. Thus he took out policy number one, in the amount of $5,000, which happened to
be the maximum amount that Provident sold without
reinsuring through another company. There were certain categories of persons, however, who could not have
bought a $500 policy at any price. According to the rate
book of 1917, among those excluded were "aeronauts,
beer bottlers, circus employees, fishermen on the high
seas, jockeys, motion picture actors, saloon keepers,
sheep herders, and snuff makers." Albert S. Caldwell,
a local insurance executive, took charge of the Life
Department, but his tenure proved brief; in 1923 he
left to accept appointment as Tennessee's Commissioner of Insurance and Banking.

With the elimination of debit insurance and the addition of life insurance, Provident's line-up of production
departments became fixed at four: Payorder, Accident,
Railroad, and Life. Increasingly, these departments assumed a semi-autonomous status within the company,
each department having its own budget, policies and
agenda. As a result, Provident operated as four companies in one.

The nation's entry into World War I posed a threat
to Provident, which had written slightly over $1.1 mil-
lion of ordinary and group life. National conscription
had begun, and mobilization was underway. Faced
with the likelihood of death on a mass scale, Provident's directors, following the lead of the insurance
industry, acted to screen out war risks. All applicants
between the ages embraced by the Selective Service

Act of 1917 were denied, and others were excluded if they contemplated enlistment.

With the insurance industry out of the business of insuring war risks, the federal government stepped in, creating a Bureau of War Risk Insurance that provided a free $10,000 policy to each soldier and sailor on active duty. Federal intervention proved a double blessing to the insurance industry, and so to Provident. Not only did the federal program relieve the industry of underwriting war risks, but also it had the effect of increasing public awareness and acceptance of life insurance. As people grew used to thinking of life insurance as a necessity, the industry's number of policies in force nationwide climbed from 29 million in 1910 to 66 million in 1920 and to 124 million in 1930.

The Accident Department was quick to take advantage of another by-product of the war, the great Red Scare. With memories of the Russian Revolution still fresh, millions of Americans reacted hysterically when a rash of bombings and labor violence hit the nation. The conviction grew that a Bolshevik plot was underway to overthrow the government. In the resulting panic, few distinctions were drawn between genuine terrorists—who were few and pathetically inept—and socialists, pacifists and labor unionists. General Leonard Wood, Army Chief of Staff, expressed the national mood when he called for the deportation of all radicals "in ships of stone with sails of lead, with the wrath of God for a breeze and with hell for their first port." Evangelist Billy Sunday favored dispatch by firing squad. Against this backdrop, Provident issued its "Business Men's Pension Policy," designed to indemnify for injuries sustained in terrorist acts. The Philadelphia *Commercial List* hailed the policy as a "momentous advancement [against] . . . secret bomb destruction by anarchical conspirators . . . [and] fiends." But as passions cooled in late 1920, Provident quietly withdrew its policy from the market.

Six months after the declaration of war, 60 percent of Provident's male staff entered the armed services. Among them, Lieutenant Cartinhour saw duty in the unit handling war risk insurance for the American Expeditionary Force. He, like all but one of the others, chose to return to Provident upon demobilization.

*   *   *   *   *

Hardly had Provident skirted the perils of war than it faced what would be an even deadlier agent of destruction. In late 1918 influenza swept the nation. Millions fell ill, and in Chattanooga as many as 38 deaths were reported in a single day. One of every four persons in the United States and Canada fell ill; out of every 1,000 stricken, 19 died. Many undertakers ran out of coffins. A retired Provident employee, Ada Parks Krug, later recalled walking to work past bodies wrapped in sheets and stacked like firewood outside Chapman's Funeral Home. Congress appropriated $1 million in an effort to fight the scourge, but before running its course the epidemic would kill half a million Americans, nearly ten times the American losses in World War I and four times the death toll of the London Plague of 1665.

For the people of Provident, it was the most difficult time in their experience together. Undermanned because of the number of clerks out sick, the staff worked valiantly to pay claims that rolled in at more than twice the normal rate. Some employees wore around their necks little bags of asafetida, a foul-smelling plant material believed to offer protection against the disease. Medical science had nothing better to offer, for as Dr.

Fancher morosely informed the board, "No one knows where influenza comes from or where it goes."

As claims mounted alarmingly, the board took the unprecedented step of authorizing Maclellan to "sell any securities thought necessary in order to provide additional funds." Setting to his task with grim urgency, Maclellan sold off securities as rapidly as money was required to pay off skyrocketing claims. The pace of liquidation left deep inroads in Provident's surplus account, reducing it from $84,000 to $39,000, a seven-year low. But before the surplus was exhausted, the epidemic ended as mysteriously as it had begun. Everyone breathed a sigh of relief when claims began to level off in January of 1919.

In the long run, however, the epidemic proved more of a blessing than a bane to Provident. Disaster is the best advertisement for insurance, stimulating demand by reminding people of life's uncertainties. Such harrowing emblems of mortality as the Civil War and World War I won thousands of converts to insurance, and the influenza epidemic was to do the same. Soon after it ended, Provident's business picked up. By year's end premium income soared past $1 million, a jump of more than 50 percent over the previous year and the largest annual gain since the banner year of 1916.

Despite—or perhaps partly because of—war and pestilence, Provident closed out the decade with its foothold secured and its future bright. During the previous ten years the directors had seen the company's territory grow from three states to 14 and its premium income increase yearly with the regularity of a strong heartbeat. A mood of confidence prevailed in the boardroom. Where earlier the executives had balked at the expense of hiring a full-time medical officer, now they felt sufficiently confident to employ an actuary and set aside

25 percent of profits as a bonus to be distributed "share and share alike among and between" Maclellan, Cartinhour, Kirksey, Webb and LeSeuer. And where earlier Maclellan had let new employees know that the company was "small and money was hard to come by," now he was singing a different song. "Provident," he told the stockholders, "has the distinction of being the largest health and accident company in the south and is endeavoring to build the south by investing its funds at home." Although it was still a midget, as insurance companies went, the course was set for bigger things.

4

Branching Out and Taking Hold

IN THE 1920s the American economy entered what some were calling a "new era." It was a time of easy money, rising productivity and frenzied finance. The stock market threatened to replace baseball as the national pastime. It was a good time to be in the insurance business. As incomes rose, more people had more to protect and more money for protection. Looking into the future, Maclellan told the stockholders, "There never has been a time in the company's history when the outlook was brighter."

The expanding economy gave Provident growing room, and grow it did. Premium income had topped $1 million in 1919 and kept on climbing. Shooting for the second million, Maclellan and Cartinhour launched a promotional contest aimed at spurring on the agents to feats of production in 1922. "One Third More—It Can Be Done!" trumpeted the contest announcement, which read like the proclamation of a general to his troops on the eve of battle:

> The big *offensive* starts April 1st. You have seven days to prepare for it. We want every man to have as his goal ONE THIRD MORE production than his best record. Take *stock* each Saturday night and determine for yourself if you have made *good* your weekly quota. If not, make it up during the *incoming* week. MAKE GOOD OR MAKE ROOM!

For those who made good, there was room—and prizes. The top producer in each department won a tailor-made suit of his choice. To the fourth-place finisher went a Stetson hat, two Manhattan shirts and a dozen pairs of silk socks.

Those who fell behind soon felt the lash, administered by the editors of the *Review*. "The Morristown office went to sleep. This won't do, boys. Come clean now and let us have something snappy for March," scolded the editors. Go-getters came in for praise befitting the exploits of a Paul Bunyan or a Pecos Bill: "Keller Albert had the biggest production of any man in the commercial department last month. He is a rip-snorting, high-rolling, bucking broncho." Invoking the Muse herself, the company offered $5 for the best poem about the contest, and among the submissions was this ode to production:

> Pettit walks the tracks
> Writing whites and blacks
> He says he'll get his ONE THIRD MORE
> If he has to walk to Baltimore.

The contest paid off handsomely. When sales figures were totted up, Maclellan announced to the assembled stockholders that gains in premium income exceeded those of any previous year. Pleased with this showing, the executive committee voted a bonus of one month's salary to each of the 125 employees, together with hefty stipends to the top five officers covered by the "share-and-share alike" agreement.

Maclellan also used the annual meeting to reveal plans that caused the stockholders to sit up and take notice. Provident would move out of rented quarters and into a home of its own. The decision was overdue, some thought. And with good reason, for there was no denying that the company had long since outgrown its tiny walk-up offices in the James Building Annex, which, despite its charm, looked like anything but headquarters of the "largest health and accident insurance company in the south." Provident could no longer give the appearance of operating out of a doll house, the executives concluded. They felt, as J. O. Carter explained, that "if a man from Tuscaloosa came up to be an agent and saw this little hole-in-the-wall office, why, he'd think there wasn't much to the company."

To revamp Provident's image, the executive committee—composed of Maclellan, Chambliss, Llewellyn, and Cartinhour—turned to Reuben Harrison Hunt, who had made a brilliant career for himself as one of the South's leading architects. The executives had every reason to congratulate themselves on their choice. Nearly every building of consequence in Chattanooga bore the stamp of Hunt's genius. Since 1895 he had designed the Tivoli Theatre, the James Building, City Hall, the County Courthouse, the Southern Railway Terminal (later re-named the Choo-Choo), and the Memorial Auditorium, creations that earned him the title "master builder of Chattanooga."

During a series of meetings with Hunt, the executives began slowly and sometimes painfully to modify their conception of the building. They wanted a grand edifice, to be sure, but Hunt's ideas of grandeur clashed with their habitual thriftiness. At first they bought a parcel of land behind the annex, intending to erect a building fronting on Chestnut Street and facing west. But the plan was abandoned when Hunt pointed out that by orienting the building toward the city's outskirts, the company would be turning its back on the heart of Chattanooga.

Next, they purchased adjoining land, thinking to

raze the annex and build an office tower in its place. The design they had in mind was functional but plain. Hunt argued against building what would be little more than a corporate warehouse, blank and characterless as a grain elevator. Instead, he proposed to build an architectural *tour de force,* its strong lines and eye-catching design expressing the spirit of a vigorous company moving confidently ahead. Hunt's proposal must have been compelling, because in January of 1923 the executive committee accepted his magnificent and costly design. It called for a monumental structure, a nine-story tower thrusting upward from a three-story base, formed by extending the intricately carved and ornamented annex 120 feet along Broad Street. In this way the old building would become an integral part of the new one, a symbolically apt arrangement for a company that seemed always to be changing, yet leaving nothing behind.

Early in February the committee received bids from five construction companies and accepted the low bid of $318,585. In March, workers broke ground, laid foundations and began hoisting steel beams and girders. Eight months and $300,000 later, a bankrupt construction company abandoned the job. Suddenly and by default, Provident was in the construction business. For the next nine months, as construction went forward under the company's control, sessions of the executive committee could have been mistaken for meetings of office builders. Talk often shifted from indemnities and annuities to the merits of various boilers, elevators and conduits. Frequently the committeemen visited building supply stores, where Cartinhour, Maclellan and the others sized up doorknobs, lavatories and weather stripping. Tiresome as the job was, they were consoled by the fact that the building, unlike those erected by professional contractors, would express their tastes down to the smallest detail.

Provident's building project was but one of thousands underway from coast to coast. In Manhattan and Chicago, skyscrapers grew like mushrooms after a rain. In Florida, developers were turning swamps into retirement communities. One edition of the Miami *Daily News,* choked with real estate advertisements, ran to 504 pages. To finance the building boom there developed a lively and lucrative market in first mortgages. For those with the money to invest, mortgage lending offered returns higher than all but the most speculative investments. Gradually, Provident increased its mortgage lending, from $311,000 in 1921 to $1.9 million in 1929.

According to textbooks of the day, a lender should lend money solely on the basis of the borrower's character, collateral and capacity. Perhaps Provident's executives never bothered to read the textbooks or, what seems more likely, chose to write their own. In any case, they saw to it that lending yielded more than interest income on the next quarter's bottom line. Thus, they lent the Clinchfield & Ohio Railroad $30,000, and, not coincidentally, the C & O granted Provident a franchise to sell accident insurance to its brakemen, engineers and machinists. Loans opened doors to Provident salesmen at the Roane Iron Company and the Calhoun Yarn Mills as well.

The executives, particularly Maclellan, also viewed credit policy as an extension of personnel policy. Showing a fatherly concern for the workforce, Maclellan customarily addressed them as "members of the Provident family," and during the depths of the depression, when the company discontinued its Christmas bonus, each employee received Maclellan's personal check for

$5. Maclellan likewise saw to it that Provident's conventions reproduced as nearly as possible the atmosphere of a family gathering. Agents took all meals together in private dining rooms, stayed in accommodations reserved exclusively for the company's use, and toured the sights as a group. It was not surprising, then, that Provident financed many a house for faithful members of the family.

J. O. Carter kept close watch over the real estate portfolio, flatly rejecting any loan applications that fell short of the company's rigorous credit standards. Some financial institutions, enticed by the six percent return on real estate loans, were offering 80 percent financing, but not Provident, which lent no more than half the appraised value of the property. Carter, made treasurer in 1928, was an exacting and jealous guardian of the company's assets. On more than one occasion he set off for home after a long evening's work at the office only to stop short, tormented by doubts: "Say, did I lock the vault? Did I lock the door?" Back he went to make doubly sure. His hard work and compulsive attention to detail paid off. Not only did the return on mortgage lending grow at an average rate of 20 percent a year, but also in 1926 Maclellan could report that "not one dollar of principal or interest" had been lost.

Equally impressive results came from L. N. Webb's Claims Department, which operated on the principle set down by Thomas Maclellan that a Provident policy was a covenant with the customer, not a contract to be probed for loopholes should the customer attempt to collect. "Our business is not a skin game," Webb liked to say. "Our purpose is to pay, not defeat, claims." The facts bore him out. Of the 48,000 claims handled in 1926, only three ended up in court. At the same time, the company retained some 50 percent of collected premiums. Webb, an affable man who never met a stranger, handled people with the same finesse as he handled claims. His knack for massaging bruised egos proved handy in a company where the spirit of competition ran high, where "Make Good or Make Room!" was no joke. The third man in the executive triumvirate, Webb operated as the corporate peacemaker.

As the summer of 1924 drew to a close, the new Provident Building stood ready for occupancy. The Chattanooga *News* called it a "monument to courage," an apt judgment in view of the fact that the executives had tied up in the building $640,000, a whopping one-third of the company's assets. Never before had they ventured so much on a single project. Nonetheless, the building promised to pay for itself many times over. Even while under construction, it had generated more favorable publicity for Provident, Maclellan declared, than the company had seen in the previous ten years. The *News,* which had recently borrowed $20,000 from Provident, was especially diligent in drawing public notice to the building and the company behind it. Reporters ransacked classical antiquity for images that would do justice to the opulent addition to Chattanooga's skyline. "Such a structure might have graced the main drags of Rome," declared one reporter. To another, the lobby so strongly suggested a "Greek temple" that he half expected a "bevy of barefoot dancers to come waltzing down the stairs." In two "Provident Extras," each running to 16 pages, the *News* spread the word of Provident's success, which was by no means common knowledge, even in the Chattanooga area.

On October 17, 1924, the executives opened the revolving brass doors to the public, and a crowd of 5,000 filed past the twin Ionic columns, through the massive arched portal and into the marble-walled lobby, where three high-speed elevators, finished inside like Pullman cars, waited to deliver them to the company's offices on the second and third floors. On the floors above were 150 other offices, soon to be occupied by some of the city's more prominent doctors, dentists and attorneys. Other tenants having interests in common with Provident filled the ground floor: the Morris Plan Bank (the future Pioneer Bank) moved into the north wing; Western Union set up shop in Provident's old quarters in the south wing; and the Chickamauga Trust Company, a mortgage lending bank that did a brisk business with the company's investment department, took an office off the main lobby.

When darkness fell, workmen trained powerful search beams on the 12-story building, lighting it up from column to cornice so that the building itself seemed to emit a luminous glow. For years to come, the Provident Building served as the company's trademark, appearing on letterheads, advertisements and policies, a symbol of the company that built it.

Along with its new building, Provident also acquired three new directors whose names were spoken with reverence in business circles. There was Paul J. Kruesi, who had grown up in Menlo Park, New Jersey, where his father, a Swiss immigrant, built Thomas Edison's first phonograph. Coming south to Chattanooga in 1902, Kruesi organized the American Lava Corporation, a manufacturer of electro-chemical products and an economic force in the community. The second new face belonged to William E. Brock, soon to be named a U.S. Senator. Starting out as a travelling salesman for the R. J. Reynolds Tobacco Company, Brock managed to trade his sample case for a candy factory, which prospered and grew into the Brock Candy Company. The third newcomer, Richard Hardy, had the unusual distinction of being namesake of a city, nearby Richard City, which owed its existence to Hardy's giant Dixie Portland Cement Company. These new directors, all financial movers and shakers, considerably strengthened Provident's ties with local business.

Looking on as these well-heeled directors met in Provident's imposing boardroom, the casual observer might have concluded, quite reasonably, that the company was in the business of selling gilt-edged securities to the very rich. Nothing could have been farther from the truth. Most of Provident's customers, now some 100,000 strong, still sweated out a living in the industrial trenches: the coal mines, lumber camps, railroad yards and steel mills. They made their homes in towns with names like Blackwater, Copperhill, Hazard, Panther Creek, Wartburg and Red Ash. They bought insurance against the economic hardships resulting from mine explosions, train derailments, gunshot wounds, pellagra, malaria and black lung. Many of them lived in houses papered with newspapers, patched with cardboard and huddled together in bleak company towns. On Saturday nights in the coal-mining town of Pocahontas, Virginia, they kept 27 saloons jumping with fist fights and gunplay.

Theirs was a world apart. And the Provident agents who entered this world were a special breed, men such as Joe Boring, a coal miner himself before becoming Provident's man in Harlan, Kentucky. "If you were in a tight spot," said a colleague of his, "you would want Joe by your side." His bushy brows and commanding presence reminded people of John L. Lewis, president of the United Mine Workers of America. The resemblance served Boring well in rough and tumble Harlan—"Bloody Harlan," as the nation's press dubbed it after labor violence there left scores wounded and dead. Frank Fitzgerald, Provident agent and one-time Harlanite, captured the essence of the place when he commented, "Harlan County is a great place to mind your own business."

Because of the recurring strikes and lockouts, the insurance agent walked a tightrope between labor and management. It was like doing business with the feuding Hatfields and McCoys. Yet Joe Boring discovered a practical way around the dilemma; he handled the coal operators while his brother Wilbur, a card-carrying U.M.W. member, dealt with the unionized miners. The work was not without its moments of black humor. Recalling one policyholder who "died by the gunshot route," Boring went on to relate that when the widow came to his office to pick up the claim check, "I tried to offer sympathy, telling her I was mighty sorry her husband lost his life, but that I was glad to be able to be of some service to her and her children. She looked down at the check and said, 'Mister, if that check is good, Charlie is worth a lot more to me dead than he was alive.' "

In the hills and hollows of North Carolina and the Virginias, John Cummings and I. E. Cooper took Provident's protection to remote lumber camps and sawmills. Cummings, an Englishman and an engineer by training, wrote applications for sawmill hands whose full names were "Doc" or "Red" and who signed with a labored X. When asked for their birthdates, many could only answer vaguely, such as, "Grandma said I was born during the big freeze." The underwriters back in the home office would have been horrified to learn that the birthdates on these applications were products of Cumming's guesswork.

In the pine barrens of West Virginia, buzz-saw operators with faces creased like old road maps paid their dimes and quarters for what they called "Cooper's insurance." For them, I. E. Cooper *was* Provident. A crack shot, Cooper put bear steaks on the table at Provident's conventions, as well as more spiritous products of the Virginia mountains. Impish John Neligan, remarking on the medicinal properties of Cooper's moonshine, claimed that the fiery liquid had "cauterized" his ulcer.

In Huntington, West Virginia, Harlow H. Huddleston supervised sales in the coal country. Robert E. Smith and his army of sub-agents wrote applications and paid claims in the mines around Bluefield, Virginia. John McGeever, a big red-faced Irishman, worked the blast furnaces and coke ovens of Birmingham. S. P. Catron and Robert L. McLemore walked the tracks, selling policies to the men of the C & O Railroad. And Bill Wood, who had lost both feet in a derailment, made a selling point of his disability as he solicited railroadmen.

These and countless other Provident fieldmen blazed the trail of acceptance for accident and health insurance as the right of every working man. To one observer in 1924, their adventures in the lonely outposts of commerce recalled America's frontier past. "The Provident man," wrote James Washington Kirksey, hard-driving chief of the Payorder Department, "takes a fast train to a station deep in the mountains, transfers to a [shuttle train] running on a catch-as-catch-can sort of schedule. Frequent derailments are expected and encountered. Then he gets out and walks. In some districts he follows trails where the last stand of the wildcat and bobcat is made. If he is lucky, he gets a berth in the company bunkhouse for the night. He rarely knows where he will sleep or eat. He is now among those he serves. His personality must please the men about him; he must know how to meet their moods and questions. His reputation must be such that he is trusted by both men and management, his disposition such that he meets hardships cheerfully; and, above all, he must keep the vision of service always before him.

"He gets the applications and carries the claim checks to relieve those who have met with misfortunes since his last visit. In this modern world of asphalt streets, steam-heated apartments, radio, petting parties and garter flasks, his story holds perhaps the last touch of pioneer realism."

This shift from rugged individualism to mass culture was nowhere more apparent than on America's streets and highways. While the fieldmen rode shuttle trains and mules, most of the nation was travelling by car. During the '20s, America's love affair with the automobile blossomed. Between 1900 and 1929, Detroit's production rose from 4,000 to 4 million cars a year. With traffic fatalities and injuries increasing apace, the Accident Department, headed by Marshall LeSueur, wrote 15,000 policies covering loss of life and limb. As a result, the claims register recorded fewer cases of mules kicking men and more cases such as this one: "S. A. Jones, Imporia, Va., Jitney Driver. Cranking car, car backfired, causing injury to hand."

From insuring people against cars to insuring the cars themselves was but a step, and Provident took it in 1922. Although the market was ripe, nobody at Provident knew the first thing about insuring property, which is as different from insuring people as needlepoint is from counterpoint. Not to be deterred, the executives imported outside talent in the person of David R. Neilson, and under his direction the Automobile Liability Department was formed to sell collision and property damage insurance. Sales brochures warned of vehicular carnage: "Day by day mad cars [are] plunging across city sidewalks to crush pedestrians against store walls. Cars are daily, hourly, momentarily running into each other." Only too true, as it turned out. The department's losses mounted until, in 1924, the executives disbanded it. Characteristically, they had decided to take their losses rather than wager heavily on a line of coverage outside the mainstream of Provident's business.

On more familiar ground, the business of insuring people, the company showed gains in every department in 1925. Closing out its 15th year since reorganizing as a stock company in 1910, Provident's premium income had increased by leaps and bounds, from $214,000 in 1910 to $3.3 million in 1925. Assets, too, had risen, from $175,000 to $2.7 million during the same span. And the half-nickel-a-day coverage, once the company's mainstay, had been replaced by such complex products as the "Five-in-One Protection Plan," which cost a man of thirty-five $1 a day and provided him with $17,500 in life insurance, $35,000 in accident insurance, $200 a month as accident or sickness indemnity, and $175 a month in case of total and permanent disability.

But while production underwriting and financial muscle had grown, Provident's marketplace had not. In 1925, as in 1915, its operations were confined by and large to the Southeast. Not only was the company isolated from the great industrial centers north of the Ohio and west of the Mississippi, but also its fortunes depended heavily on southern business cycles. To make matters worse, several large northern-based insurance companies, including the Northwestern Mutual Life and the Inter-Ocean, were re-entering the South after an absence of 25 years or more. Taken together, these facts meant that Provident needed to grow beyond its regional base. This it did, in 1926, thanks largely to Carl Cartinhour.

Physically as well as intellectually imposing, Cartinhour invited respect, if not intimacy. His cold and penetrating gaze made subordinates feel that they had better say what they had to say fast and that it had better be right. He combined the analytical powers of a chess master with the directness of a rhinoceros. His ability to stay several moves ahead of the game was uncanny, as more than a few wayward agents learned. On one occasion an agent whom Lady Luck had deserted wired the company for a $100 advance, which was granted. Two days later the agent wired again, asking for another advance. He received instead a telegram that read: "Make them use a new deck or play with their sleeves rolled up. (signed) W. C. Cartinhour." In a reflective mood, he once commented that "every company needs at least one S.O.B. to make sure things get done. I guess I'm the S.O.B. here."

In April of 1926, following four months of negotiation, Cartinhour closed a deal that opened the West to Provident. Under the agreement, Provident bought the entire railroad insurance business of the Detroit-based Standard Accident Company. This included $500,000 in premium collections from 25,000 railroad workers and, better still, franchises in eight states that formed a series of stepping stones to the Pacific coast: Michigan, Minnesota, Wisconsin, Kansas, Iowa, Montana, Oregon and Washington. Provident would ride the rails to the coast, and to speed it along Cartinhour brought in Standard Accident's Harry Conley, a squat, round-face and feisty Irishman, who took over the Railroad Department.

An aura of romance and power still clung to the rails. There were people living who could yet remember when the railway czars changed the way America told time. The year was 1883. The Harriman and Vanderbilt interests, finding it a nuisance to schedule trains in a nation divided into dozens of time zones, lobbied Congress into enacting Standard Time, or "railroad time," as it was popularly known. People took to the streets in protest, shouting "Damn old Vanderbilt! Give us back our time!" But the railroads prevailed. Railroadmen, like members of many other powerful industries, were clannish; they called their union a "brotherhood." They spoke two languages, "one of which was English," said Harry Conley. To sell them insurance, an agent had to be bilingual, and Conley specialized in this. He brought to Provident a sophisticated understanding of railroadmen and a network of contacts built up during his 24-year career with Standard Accident.

Other departments soon secured footholds in the West, with Life opening an agency in Los Angeles and Payorder entering Kansas. By 1928, when licenses were obtained to do business in California, Colorado, Nebraska, North Dakota and Idaho, Provident's geographic reach extended to 34 of the then 48 states.

The West had been opened, but the executives were of two minds on the matter of developing it. Cartinhour took the activist line, Maclellan the gradualist. Cartinhour, who played poker with relish and skill, believed in taking the well-calculated risk every now and then. Maclellan, who did not play cards, believed in waiting patiently for the sure thing. Neither man dictated corporate policy. Rather, the interplay of their opposing viewpoints shaped policy in the long run. For the time being, though, the company would move west gradually, deliberately. Emphasizing the point, Maclellan informed the directors that Provident's policy was to "develop as far as possible in the states at home, only making contracts in states at a distance where general agents can be secured capable of developing the company's business without detailed supervision." As proof of its commitment to home base, Provident would, Maclellan added, invest in local mortgages and bonds an amount "at least equal" to the premiums paid by Chattanoogans.

The four vice presidents, each of whom ran his department as if it were a small company of his own, regularly competed for the honor of setting the year's production record. All aggressive achievers, none was more so than Kirksey. Not to be outdone entirely by the Railroad Department's success, Kirksey went looking for a major new account. What he turned up, in October of 1926, was the Pocahontas Fuel Corporation, which controlled the biggest and richest deposits of bituminous coal in the nation. On his 17th anniversary with Provident, Kirksey won an exclusive franchise from Pocahontas Fuel to insure its 5,000 workers. The resulting premiums amounted to $100,000 annually, easily Provident's largest single account.

Because of the rapid advances made by the Railroad and Payorder departments, Maclellan pronounced 1926 "the best year in the company's history." Each of the four departments boasted income of $1 million, which in the not so distant year of 1919 had represented the company's total income.

Provident was growing not only in resources but also in personnel. There were more than 150 employees in Chattanooga, underwriting applications and processing claims generated by 1,650 field agents. On the recommendation of an efficiency expert, bells were installed in the home office to ring in the workday, to announce ten-minute recesses morning and afternoon, and to signal quitting time. But the end-of-work bell did not toll for everyone. Bookkeepers toiled over their ledgers until they balanced to the penny; executives met with agents late into the night, hammering out contracts that kept both the underwriters and the client happy; secretaries typed and re-typed special contracts for fretful agents who needed to catch the last train. As one veteran put it: "We sometimes stayed until 9:00 or 9:30—without overtime—running the old adding machines that went *clonk, clonk!* We just thought of the long hours as a regular part of the job."

Despite the sometimes grueling pace, the employees still knew how to have a good time. They proved it at the annual banquet of 1926, held three days after Christmas in the Silver Ballroom of Chattanooga's landmark Read House Hotel. Everyone was there, from the mailroom boys to the top brass. Formality was thrown to the winds, or at least suppressed as much as possible in an organization where women still showed up for work each day wearing white gloves. Paul Ray, head of the Life Department, startled the crowd when he stormed into the hall disguised as a Swedish farmer, shouting in the thick brogue of his ancestry. His message was that Thurman Payne, of the Chattanooga general agency, had hoodwinked him into buying a policy, and he wanted his money back. The Charleston was the dance of the year, and the Read House waiters did it with such abandon that those in the back of the room stood on their chairs to watch. J. O. Carter shook the chandeliers with his resonant baritone voice; Helen Metcalfe, of the Payorder Department, costumed as an Italian fruit vendor, gave her rendition of "Carlotta Mia"; and John Neligan

played the air-saxophone, puffing until he was blue
in the face, while a real saxophonist played behind
the curtain.

Just what song Neligan coaxed out of his air-saxophone is unknown, but no song could have been more
in tune with the times than "We're In the Money." During the last three years the number of Americans who
paid tax on incomes of $1 million or more had nearly
quadrupled. Stock prices rose day by day, month by
month, convincing many people that the nation was
on its way to a "permanent plateau of prosperity." In
an article entitled "Everybody Ought to Be Rich," John
J. Raskob, chairman of General Motors' finance committee, argued in the pages of *Ladies' Home Journal*
that anybody who saved $15 a month and bought sound
common stocks would in 20 years be worth $80,000.
It seemed logical enough, at the time.

As economic activity doubled or tripled yearly,
Provident stepped up its efforts to win new business.
The Life Department, guided by Paul Ray, opened
agencies in Raleigh, Louisville, Des Moines and Baltimore. Life insurance in force topped $35 million. In
April 1929, Cartinhour and Kirksey negotiated the purchase of the Meridian Insurance Company, of Charleston, West Virginia, an acquisition that added $300,000
in premiums.

Later that year the Chattanooga *News* ran a story
headlined: "Provident Gets Largest Health and Accident Contract in U.S." The contract, landed by Harry
Conley, covered all 65,000 employees of the Southern
Railroad and its affiliates. Translated into dollars and
cents, the contract was worth a staggering $1 million
in annual premiums. But before it became effective
on November 1, events on Wall Street would change
the way America—and Provident—did business.

5

Through Panic and Depression

B LACK THURSDAY, October 24, 1929. Panic broke
out in the canyons of Wall Street when waves of
"Sell!" orders suddenly hit the New York Stock Exchange. Stock prices, driven ever upward during years
of wild speculation, collapsed as investors dumped
more than 12 million shares into a market where buyers had all but disappeared. Brokers scrambled to call
loans and to liquidate portfolios at a fraction of opening
prices. The tickers chattered ceaselessly, but ran hours
behind the trading. In office buildings up and down
the Street, lights burned far into the night while har-
ried clerks sifted through the avalanche of transactions, looking for the bottom line.

Asked to comment on the disaster, Thomas W. La-
mont, Sr., partner in the redoubtable J. P. Morgan and
Company, passed it off as a "little distress selling on
the stock exchange." More followed on October 29. U.S.
Steel, organized and backed by the House of Morgan
itself, resumed a long slide that would take it from
262 to 22. Another blue chip, Montgomery Ward, was
on its way from 138 to 4. Other, less solid stocks would
depreciate to virtually nothing, despite bullish predictions from Wall Street.

In Chattanooga, as in cities across the nation, businessmen watched the unfolding drama for clues to its
eventual effect on the local economy. Provident's first

response, like that of other local financial institutions, was official silence. Even during closed meetings of the board and the executive committee, no one ventured a comment for the record. Only in its internal publication did the company openly acknowledge the disaster, and then to point a moral rather than risk a prediction. "Wall Street Teaches A Lesson," ran the headline emblazoned in 20-point type across the front page of the November *Review.* "Never before in history," the text went on, "has there been anything like . . . the recent Crash on Wall Street. Stock values went down like the *Titanic.* . . . Small traders were wiped out and millionaires were reduced to beggary.

"That shows what can happen to stocks. The man who plans on leaving his widow and children a fortune of such uncertain and fluctuating value is simply kidding himself and them."

But, as the *Review* was quick to point out, "there is one sure estate that can be created—Life Insurance. The stock market may rise and fall as it will; the Bulls and Bears can fight till they devour each other—the Life Insurance policy tucked away in the strong box will always be worth its full value."

Provident had followed an investment policy every bit as conservative as the one it was urging on the public. The company's portfolio contained not a share of common stock. But even gilt-edged securities depreciated under the fierce deflationary pressures triggered by the Crash. Wages, dividends, salaries—practically everything was going down except unemployment. Particularly hard hit were mortgage loans, of which Provident held $1.9 million. As early as December, hardpressed borrowers had fallen in arrears, and on February 17, 1930 the executives began calling some of these real estate loans, demanding a reduction of principal on others, and, in some cases, foreclosing on property. Foreclosure was used as a last resort, according to A. C. (Gus) Bryan, who took over the mortgage lending operation from J. O. Carter in 1935. "Preservation of principal was the main objective," Bryan later explained. "If a borrower couldn't pay the interest, we tried to get him to pay the real estate taxes. If he couldn't pay the taxes, we sometimes advanced the taxes in order to keep the property occupied and thereby prevent vandalism and deterioration."

When such efforts proved less than uniformly successful, Provident wound up holding unlikely properties scattered across the Southeast. In time, Bryan and Carter found themselves responsible for looking after a gasoline station in Miami, a tobacco farm in North Carolina, orange groves in central Florida and even a cattle ranch in Texas. Nevertheless, the two money managers held foreclosures to roughly ten percent of the total value of mortgage loans.

Safeguarding these and other investments loomed as "management's greatest problem," said Cartinhour. So critical was the need for expert counsel that the finance committee, composed of Maclellan, Cartinhour, Chambliss and Carter, broke with tradition and invited an outside director to join their deliberations. The director, Scott L. Probasco, owned controlling interest in the stately American Trust and Banking Company, besides which he had reputedly once made $1 million on a single, shrewdly-timed transaction involving a textile mill. Even his detractors admitted respect for Probasco's financial savvy.

Probasco and the others acted to fortify Provident's already strong financial position against any eventuality short of revolution. They sharply curtailed mortgage lending, placed the bulk of funds in low yielding but liquid government bonds, and spread remaining funds among short-term bonds of telephone, electric and tobacco companies. Come what might, the directors reasoned, people would continue to smoke, talk on the telephone and read by electric light. The finance committee also pruned away weak or worthless securities that might cause financial analysts to give the company anything other than its customary excellent ratings. Among the write-offs was $25,000 in bonds of Insull Utilities Investments, whose founder, Samuel Insull, had risen from a five-shilling-a-week clerk in London to become lord and master of a Chicago-based holding company which controlled a vast network of utilities stretching from Maine to Texas. In 1928 it was "worth a million dollars to be seen talking to Sam Insull in front of the Continental Bank," wrote one newspaperman, perhaps only half jokingly. But Insull's empire, built on leverage and kept aloft by inflated stock, promptly crumpled under the stress of depression, and he fled the country when indicted for criminal mismanagement of Insull Utilities Investments.

By writing off dubious securities of this sort, Provident earned the praise of insurance commissioners. After one examination of the company's books, the commissioners of Tennessee, Nebraska and Virginia reported that Provident's "management is to be especially commended for its practice of voluntarily charging down to a sound basis any assets of doubtful value." Out of this new emphasis on financial affairs grew an Investment Department, staffed with professional money managers who would guide the company's increasingly complex financial policy in the years to come.

Elsewhere in the organization, equally significant changes had been set in motion or accelerated by the depression. Unemployment, which claimed 100,000 additional jobs each week, exacted a particularly grim toll among workers in the steel, coal, lumber and railroad industries. Trains ran less frequently and were noticeably shorter, the sky over Birmingham's steel mills grew clear, and coal production was headed for its lowest ebb since 1898. By the middle of 1931, Provident's premium income, more than 80 percent of which came from workers in these sorely afflicted industries, showed a marked decline. Even in the Payorder Department, always the company's big money maker, collections ran 15 percent behind the previous year.

As traditional business contracted, however, an opportunity arose to expand in a new, potentially profitable direction. In August, Carl Cartinhour learned that the accident insurance department of the Southern Surety Company, in Des Moines, was for sale. This fact would not have elicited Cartinhour's interest four years earlier, when Southern Surety's assets far exceeded Provident's income. But that was before Rogers Caldwell, a high-rolling investment banker out of Nashville, gained control of the Iowa-based casualty company. By then Caldwell was on his way to assembling a financial empire of more than 50 interlocking companies worth upwards of $650 million—on paper. To keep this debt-heavy conglomerate afloat, he shuffled assets from company to company faster than the eye—or regulatory agencies—could see. Southern Surety, like other captive subsidiaries, found itself required to swap bankable securities for the junk bonds peddled by Caldwell and Company. The jerry-built structure flew to pieces when the stock market lurched out of control. Bankrupt, Southern Surety was put on the auction block. The Home Insurance Company, of New York, snapped up its casualty business. Its accident

business could be had for 24¢ on the dollar, Cartinhour
told the executive committee. He championed the purchase, arguing that it would provide new sources of
income at a time when old accounts were drying up.

On September 1, 1931, Provident paid $240,000 and
received policies worth $1 million in annual premi-
ums, together with Southern Surety's network of 1,900
agents in the Midwest and on the Pacific coast, where
Provident was still thin on the ground. Better still, Provident acquired a strong accident department staff, including Southern's agency manager, a brilliant, brash
and ambitious young man by the name of James E.
Powell. No one made much of the connection at first,
least of all Powell, who left Des Moines with the sink-
ing feeling that he was "being sold down the river."
With the raffish good looks of an Errol Flynn, Powell
seemed miscast for the part of small-town insurance
executive. What attracted and eventually seduced him,
though, was the chance to create an Accident Department after his own fashion; Provident's had always
limped along behind the Payorder Department. After
management gave Powell a free hand, he would take
the department to the forefront of the accident and
health insurance industry.

At the end of 1931, Provident registered a four percent drop in premium income, a better showing than
could have been expected without the business brought
in through Southern Surety. Still, there was no cause
for jubilation. Banks were going down at the rate of
45 a week, taking with them the savings of thousands
of depositors, many of whom then turned to insurance
companies for policy loans. And with nearly a third
of the nation out of work, disability claims and policy
lapses soared. Concluding his annual report on an un-

characteristically gloomy note, Maclellan said simply, "For 1932 it is impossible to make predictions."

Faced with uncertainty at every turn, Maclellan ordered the first of two salary reductions, ranging from ten percent for the top brass to five percent for the lowest echelons. In addition, "all development expenses that might be worthwhile in years of prosperity" were cut to the bone. And to forestall policy lapses, the company encouraged policyholders to accept reductions in benefits that would translate into lower premium payments.

Despite reverses and retrenchment, the company was breaking new ground. Most notably, Kirksey's Payorder Department had carried Provident into two industries beyond the traditional coal, steel, lumber and railroad accounts. First to come was the textile industry. Although Payorder had insured a handful of textile workers as early as 1918, it was not until 1929 that Kirksey decided to push this business in earnest. His decision, timed as it was, undoubtedly grew in part from the fact that during the 1920s northern mill owners had moved south in force, bringing a degree of stability to what had been a volatile and, for an insurer, a treacherous regional industry. Then, in 1929, an insurance broker from North Carolina, Robert U. Woods, approached Kirksey with the novel idea of selling hospital-surgical insurance to textile workers in Rutherford County, North Carolina. So far as either of them knew, this had never before been attempted. Yet circumstances in Rutherford County seemed to favor the plan. The depression had come early there; few mill-hands could afford hospital care. More to the point, though, the local hospital had been driven to the verge of bankruptcy for want of paying patients. Its director,

Dr. Robert Crawford, was naturally eager to throw his considerable influence behind a hospital-surgical plan, if only some company would offer it. "If you'll write it," Crawford told Kirksey, "I'll see that you get into the mills."

Kirksey was game, and in August of 1929 Provident began insuring workers at the Carolina Cotton and Woolen Mill, a subsidiary of Marshall Field, located in Spray, North Carolina. A first for Provident, the deal may well have been a milestone in the history of insurance as well. Clarence Griffin, director of North Carolina's Department of Archives and History during the 1940s, judged it to be the "first insurance contract written by an insurance company for the employees of a specific employer covering hospital and surgical benefits."

The plan caught on so quickly that only a few months passed before Provident had insured virtually all the millhands in Rutherford County. From there the plan spread through North Carolina and Georgia, into mills owned by Burlington Industries, Collins and Aikman, and the Goodyear Tire and Rubber Company. The plan spawned a new crop of Provident agents, who made it their business to know the textile industry inside out. Among them were Elton Kirksey, son of J. W. and a smooth operator who "knew all the connections and how to put them together"; John W. Parks, a crack salesman who often berated home office officials in letters salted with terms such as "knucklehead" and "lame brain," but invariably closed with his "kindest personal regards"; and Robert Gordon, a man of wit and charm who, once asked by higher-ups to list the attributes of a successful Payorder agent, responded with this definition: "He must be a night owl able to work all day and drive all night and appear fresh the next day. He must learn to sleep on the floor and eat two meals a day to economize on expenses so he can entertain friends in the next town. He must be an expert driver, talker, dancer, traveler, bridge player, poker-hound, golf player, diplomat, financier, capitalist, philanthropist and an authority on palmistry, psychology, physiology, dogs, cats and horses." He must, in short, be all things to all men, or at least spend his energy and personality freely in cultivating business executives who, taken as a group, might have little in common apart from the power to grant Provident a franchise to sell insurance. Cultivating these executives sometimes placed unusual demands on an agent. Once, Gordon was in the middle of soliciting tobacco baron Arch Taylor when Taylor, seated at the far end of the table, took a man-size chew of tobacco and then casually slid the plug and a pocket knife down to Gordon. Eyeing it doubtfully, Gordon allowed that he didn't believe he cared for a chew, thank you.

"Sissy, huh?" Taylor drawled.

Cornered, Gordon took a small chew, or what seemed like a small chew, until "it got bigger and bigger and I got sicker and sicker," he recalled. But rising to the occasion, Gordon walked away with a franchise to sell insurance at the Taylor Tobacco Company.

Salesmanship was elevated to an art form by another Payorder agent, Edward L. Mitchell—known as "Billy" to scores of friends who would one day include such textile kings as Roger Milliken, of Deering-Milliken; Joe Lanier, of West Point Pepperell; J. Spencer Love, of Burlington Industries; and Walter Montgomery, of Spartan Mills. In 1933, though, Mitchell started work as a $25-a-week solicitor, assigned to the Richmond Hosiery Mill. Never having been inside a mill, Mitchell found the racket of hundreds of looms deafening. The noise would drown out his sales pitch. But the mill manager refused to allow him to speak to the workers one at a time in a quieter setting. To make himself heard above the roaring looms, Mitchell had to get within kissing range of the snuff-dipping mill-hands.

"Old buddy," Mitchell shouted into their ears, "I've got a damn fine thing here if you want it."

"It's all right for them that wants it, but I don't want it," some replied.

But more often than not, Mitchell made the sale. The mill worked three shifts and so did Mitchell, slogging home red-eyed but happy at two A.M.

On top of the textile business, Kirksey's Payorder Department began adding public utilities to its growing list of clients. The idea of insuring utility workers originated in the mind of Morgan Cooper (Joe) Nichols, then safety director of the Alabama Power Company. A deeply compassionate man, Nichols had set out in 1929 to find an affordable insurance plan to cover Alabama Power's linemen, switch-pullers and repairmen against the hazards they encountered while working around hot wires and whirling dynamos. Nichols sounded out a number of insurance executives, who either stated flatly that utility workers were uninsurable or else quoted prohibitive rates. Undaunted, Nichols held to the conviction that it was possible to develop a sound plan, affordable for the worker as well as profitable to the insurer. Hearing that Provident had long specialized in writing such plans, Nichols called on Kirksey, who listened with an open mind and eventually agreed to work with Nichols in designing a plan for Alabama Power.

The resulting plan, put into effect late in 1929, proved a winner. Its most significant result, for Provident, came when Nichols decided to join the company and carry similar insurance plans to utilities in many states. In his work Nichols displayed two qualities that made for a distinguished career which would take him to the highest reaches of the Payorder Department. One was his stubborn refusal to be bound by the possible. "We were always looking for what couldn't be done," he later recalled. "The rating book was just a guide. We wrote the business and rated it at the same time. Each policy was tailored to the individual client. It was always such a challenge that you felt there was an answer somewhere and, if one thing didn't work, another might. You kept moving, refusing to be licked, until you found the combination of circumstances and coverages that got you the business." The other quality was his heartfelt conviction that in doing well for Provident he was also doing good for others. "I don't know how to put it without sounding a little sanctimonious," he explained, "but I couldn't write individual insurance. Not that there is anything wrong with it. I would go by a door a dozen times, hoping the guy was out, not wanting to call or sell him. But when you came to group insurance and you could see the people who were brought into it who would not be insured otherwise, then there was always the feeling that, by golly, this is something that has to be, this is something that is really needed." Joe Nichols—a professional businessman flying amateur colors; tough and subtle under an engaging cloak of amiability; motivated by humane feelings that he put into action, not on parade—exemplified Provident at its best.

*   *   *   *   *

In March, 1933 the nation entered its 41st month of continuous depression. In most areas businesses

merely marked time. Fifteen million workers had no
jobs, and millions more drew greatly reduced wages.
Provident's actuary, Kenneth Piper, reported to the
board another grim statistic: the Life Department
showed a sharp increase in claims resulting from suicide. Atlanta and Knoxville, their coffers empty, paid
off city employees with scrip, and Asheville declared
itself bankrupt. The banking system had gone belly
up; over 5,000 banks in 31 states were closed indefi-
nitely, their deposits of $3.4 billion out of reach of cus-
tomers. Comparatively, Provident had fared much better than the appalling conditions might have led one
to suspect. Although income was down, the company
remained rock solid. It had a ratio of $139 in assets
to each $100 in liabilities, nearly one-third larger than
the industry average. The company had borrowed not
a cent, while steadily paying claims totalling $2.3 mil-
lion at year's end. The insurance commissioner of Tennessee, after scrutinizing Provident's operations, concluded that "the affairs of the company have been
amply and conservatively administered. It has lost little business and its surplus has continued to grow in
the face of prolonged financial depression. In our opinion, it presents a strong financial structure, constituting
a high order of security to its policyholders." Another
accolade came when *Best's Insurance Reports,* the
Dun and Bradstreet of the insurance industry, rated
Provident "excellent," Best's supreme rating and one
given to fewer than a third of life insurance companies
in 1933.

In mid-year the economy showed signs of improve-
ment, owing largely to the bold and far-reaching recovery measures adopted by President Roosevelt during
his first 100 days in office. By 1934 the New Deal had
put the nation on the long road to recovery. For Maclel-

lan, the turnaround in Provident's business was "beyond anything . . . we could have anticipated a year ago." Its collections surging, Payorder closed the year with income up for the first time since 1929. And Powell's Accident Department registered a profit of $64,000. "We can say without question that the N.R.A. [National Recovery Administration] has been responsible for much of this improvement," announced Maclellan in a statement that undoubtedly caused apoplexy among some stockholders who shared Maclellan's staunch Republicanism. The worst was over, said Maclellan, declaring that "for Provident the year 1934 was the first out of the depression." The executive committee had already restored the salary cuts of the last two years, and it went so far as to award bonuses of five percent to all home office employees in 1935.

That same year the executive committee decided to reorganize the flagging Life Department, which from inception had performed below their expectations, despite the fact that the conditions under which life insurers operated had improved dramatically since Provident offered its first policy in 1917. Not only had World War I stimulated demand but also people were living longer. Advances in medicine, nutrition and the standard of living had been responsible in the first third of the 20th century for increasing American life expectancy from 49 to 51 years, for cutting infant mortality by two-thirds, and for slashing the death rate of typhoid from 36 to two per 100,000 cases. Provident's Life Department had little to show for all that, and the executive committee felt that major repairs were in order. The overhaul was entrusted to a relative newcomer who, nonetheless, had been born and bred to Provident. He was Robert Llewellyn Maclellan, grandson of Thomas Maclellan and son of Robert J. Maclel-

lan. An earnest young man with dark hair and square
jaw, Robert L. applied himself skillfully and tire-
lessly until he mastered every detail of whatever subject occupied his attention. He had been graduated
from Dartmouth, where as editor of the *Dartmouth
Pictorial,* he was forever lending money to his sub-
editor, Nelson A. Rockefeller, whose father, presum-
ably having acquired habits of thrift as a child earning an allowance by killing flies at a penny apiece,
kept Nelson on short rations. In 1928 Robert had left
the Ivy League behind, joining Provident as an auditor
in the Life Department. His connection with the company was inevitable and his advancement came to
no one's surprise. In 1935 he was made vice president and head of the Life Department.

At that time the company had $79 million of life
insurance in force, primarily group life, sold mainly
by Payorder agents. Ordinary life accounted for only
$21 million, a negligible sum even when measured
against the holdings of purely regional competitors.
There were other problems as well. To help solve them
Maclellan recruited a seasoned life insurance executive who would make his mark on the company, a full-
faced and hospitable man named Sam Miles. Content
and successful handling life agents for the Pilot Life
and Accident Insurance Company, of Greensboro,
North Carolina, Miles was at first reluctant to accept
a similar position with Provident. To do so would be
to take a step down from a large department to a tiny
one. Finally, though, it was the "challenge of building
a Life Department from the ground up" that lured him
to Provident. If ever the department were to operate
in the black, its basic strategy must change, concluded
Maclellan and Miles. Heretofore, agents of ordinary

life had sold only small policies of the sort that lapsed frequently and at great cost to the company. There was a need for business that would stay on the books, and, as Maclellan and Miles saw it, this meant going after high-income prospects. This entailed a major overhaul for, as Miles described the situation, "we didn't have the right contracts, agents or policies to go into the top market." Revamping the department was a slow and sometimes frustrating process, but Maclellan and Miles' efforts would begin to bear fruit in the 1940s. In this they were aided by actuary Kenneth Piper, office manager Ed Jones and medical director Dr. Charles R. Henry, graduate of the Emory Medical School and an avid horseman and antiquarian. It was Dr. Henry's duty to diagnose trends in mortality, a task which, by all accounts, he much preferred to diagnosing patients. Once, he was standing in Provident's lobby when, as the story goes, a young lady fainted before his eyes, whereupon Dr. Henry, momentarily at a loss, cried, "Somebody get a doctor!" It was a good story. It might even have been true.

Elsewhere, in the Accident Department, another self-improvement campaign had been launched, under the iron hand of Jim Powell. "If you don't look good, you look stupid," Powell liked to tell his agents; for him there was no middle ground. Easily driven to black rages by the merely average, Powell was not altogether pleased with his department. Upon taking charge, he found that it sold "primarily $1 policies in the cotton rows of the South." And, too, the caliber of agents occasionally left something to be desired, as he learned when policyholders out of Texas deluged the home office with letters requesting the Indian blankets that one agent had assured them Provident would send as a small token of its gratitude for their business. Nor was Powell's temper helped when an agent "got our money and his mixed up."

Even though the sluggish economy ruled out any major efforts to upgrade the department, Powell was moving to weed out incompetent agents and replace them with the hand-picked men he had brought from Southern Surety. These included Marshall Goodmanson, who in 1939 would open the department's first branch, in San Francisco; and John Campbell, soon to be Powell's man in Chicago. Powell was also running what he called the "bullpen," a metaphorical place in the department where he trained aspiring young men and then sent into the field those who showed promise. Among those whom Powell sent out to pitch were Earl Montgomery, who carved out a handsome territory for himself and Provident in Los Angeles; Todd Baker, Accident's man in Nashville; Eston V. Whelchel, a native of Chickamauga, Georgia, who acquitted himself with high honors in Newark, New Jersey; and Lafayette Davis, who opened up Atlanta in times so lean that he cultivated brokers by day and then at night loaded his wife and kids in the car and called on the school teachers who bought such small policies as kept him going. Together with James Sedgwick, Powell's aide-de-camp, this group represented some of the professionals who would, in the years to come, help Powell fulfill his dream of selling top-drawer products considerably in advance of their time.

*   *   *   *   *

In 1937 Provident turned 50, and to celebrate the occasion the elder Maclellan staged an agency convention for which 350 agents and their wives came from 35 states to Lookout Mountain. They represented the top producers out of more than 2,000 agents who sold and served Provident's half million policyholders. It was owing largely to their efforts, Cartinhour told them, that Provident's assets this year had almost reached $10 million. The stellar performance of the Payorder Department came in for much praise. In the past five years its business had increased 150 percent and now included 150,000 workers in 800 different plants: 300 coal mines, 200 lumber mills, 140 textile mills, and an array of other concerns such as the Chicago *Daily News* and Anheuser-Busch.

The Golden Jubilee Convention, held at the posh Lookout Mountain Hotel, gave everybody a chance to sound off, wax nostalgic and generally have a rollicking good time. Judge Alexander Chambliss expounded in sonorous periods on the theme of rededication to the founding principles laid down so "strongly and firmly" by Thomas Maclellan that "neither war nor pestilence nor panic" had shaken Provident's ability to meet every obligation to its policyholders. Old hands from the field stepped up to the microphone and read brief speeches which, along with other memorabilia, were solemnly sealed in a "treasure chest" to be opened 25 years thence. The conventioneers, led by J. O. Carter, sang "Provident, My Provident" to the tune of "Maryland, My Maryland." Then party hats were donned— Cartinhour looking a trifle out of character in his— and a belly dancer gyrated before the disapproving glare of some wives.

As always, though, death was no respecter of occasions. In this gala anniversary year Provident, at last practicing what it so long had preached, put in a group life program for its own employees. The first beneficiaries were the heirs of J. W. Kirksey, father of the Payorder Department, a director of the company and a man as responsible as any other for its triumphs over the past 28 years. After a lingering illness, he died on March 15, at the age of 55. For a number of years, no clear successor would emerge to fill his post. During the interim, Howard Hill was named chief of Payorder, while in fact Leslie Webb supervised most of its operations.

Kirksey's death came at a critical time for the department, just as the giants of the insurance world, Travelers, Aetna, Metropolitan and Prudential, moved into the southern textile industry. Their sudden interest in this regional industry grew out of a shift in its ownership. When the depression hit full force, northern mill owners gobbled up numerous financially distressed southern mills, forming huge chains which, in cases such as J. P. Stevens Company, stretched from Maine to Georgia. Since Travelers and the others already insured the northern segment of these chains, it seemed only natural that they should pick up the southern segment as well. After all, these insurance giants did business in such volume that they could, in theory, quote lower rates than could Provident. In that event, Provident would lose most of its 200 accounts built up since 1929. Rather than surrender to superior force, however, the Payorder Department chose to fight. The textile war was on.

On Provident's side, Joe Nichols and Billy Mitchell emerged to lead the campaign. The man who was "always looking for what couldn't be done," Nichols decided on an appropriately audacious strategy. Provident offered to bid on a textile company's entire operation, north and south. The textile executives agreed, never thinking that Provident stood a chance to underbid its large competitors, one of which, Metropolitan Life, had nearly 350 times the assets of Provident. Mitchell cozied up to the executives, yarning and drinking and fishing with them, all the while putting across the message that Provident sold service as well as insurance: "We're in Greensboro, and Rockmart, and Raleigh paying claims every day. You don't have to go to New York to find us."

With L. N. Webb's blessing, Nichols prepared bids incorporating what he called "guaranteed retention," which meant that Provident agreed to retain only so much of the premiums and rebate the balance no matter what the claim loss. Although this arrangement would later become commonplace, it was considered risky at the time, when there was no large body of statistical evidence from which to calculate the probable claim losses arising from the textile industry. Even so, Nichols was convinced that the underwriting risk posed by textile workers, like that of utility workers, was exaggerated. His competitors believed otherwise; they quoted flat premium rates higher than those submitted by Provident.

This unexpected turn of events provoked amazement in more than a few New York and Hartford boardrooms, but no one could argue with Nichols' figures. One company after another signed contracts, and by 1940 Nichols could say that Provident had retained "every single piece of business and gained several national chains." He remembered how the executives of one such chain, Deering-Milliken, reacted on first signing with Provident: "They were completely baffled. They felt like this little southern insurance company shouldn't be doing this." Equally astonished were representatives of the insurance Goliaths who had, as Mitchell put it, "come down from New York to pull strings, and when they pulled they found the little guy from Provident on the other end."

6

Time Out for War

"THIS IS THE CLOSE of my 47th day on the Anzio beachhead," wrote John Saint, on leave from Provident's Accident Department. "The first night I was with a soldier who had never seen action. A Jerry plane came down the beach, dived, dropped three. When I saw the plane I pushed this guy down on his face and followed suit. The last of the three came pretty close, the earth heaved and the concussion was terrific. When he came up the only thing he said was a very quiet, 'My God, those things will kill you!' We have laughed about it ever since. . . . This is a strange world we live in."

For John Saint, as for millions of others, World War II put an end to what had been familiar, settled and expected. Six months after Pearl Harbor more than half of Provident's male staff had answered the call to arms, and an exodus of similar proportions took place in the field. The abrupt loss of manpower disrupted operations, slowing down pre-war initiatives in the Life and Accident departments and forcing the discontinuance of one practice that had long been a point of pride in the company. Its end was foreshadowed in 1941, when a nation-wide transportation shortage compelled the company to cancel its annual convention.

The next year, as rationing diverted to the war effort vast quantities of rubber, gasoline and steel, Provident abandoned its policy of paying claims on the spot. Up until then, Webb's Claims Department, lately under the day-to-day direction of Keith Kropp and Robert Bracewell, had regularly dispatched scores of claims adjusters to settle with policyholders in person. To its customers in need, Provident was not a form letter; it was Leland Fussell and John Wesley and Joe Estes and C. H. Absher. These and other claims adjusters also protected Provident against the bane of all accident and health companies: litigious lawyers, larcenous policyholders, and doctors who turned every sore throat into a tonsillectomy and every stomach-ache into an appendectomy. The work was demanding, the hours long, and the travel far from glamorous. C. H. Absher, a grizzled veteran, left a wry account of a typical day in the life of a claims man. It reads in part: "First to receive our attention is the morning's mail [where] we find a number of claims to be investigated (invariably at the coal company where we worked yesterday) and a summons to appear in a magistrate's court to defend a case which we thought we had settled.

"[Then] we start on our day's journey, which is over a route so familiar that we have named most of the telephone posts. We now arrive at the mouth of a gorge, and after traveling over almost impassable roads for several miles, reach the office of the Hoot Owl Coal Company, where we shake hands with the management, buy the Coca-Colas or beer (this to make friends), discuss football, baseball and prizefighting for awhile, and then get down to business.

"We are advised by the payroll clerk that Pete Gastrowaski is sick and wants an advance on his insurance, and that Jack Whizzerinski received his check but thought he should have had a ticket to the World's Fair attached.

"Late in the afternoon we arrive in a coalfield town to interview some of our lawyer friends that we have been keeping up through the depression and who are now bringing suit.

"Finally we arrive at the hotel tired and dusty. Here we run into a friend and we pay for the dinners. Our friend suggests the picture show, so we sit for two hours in a stuffy room seeing 'Buck Jones, the Fighting Sheriff.' "

Such toils and travail became less common once the department began to settle the majority of claims by mail. By the time rationing ended, paying claims by mail had proved so economical that nobody suggested a return to the old ways. Although special investigators would probe dubious claims and teams of agents would pay claims at the scene of mining disasters, the days of the roving claimsmen were over.

Another change of even larger import was underway in the Payorder Department which, after a period of answering to the name "Group-Payorder," had settled on the designation "Group." This shift in terminology reflected a profound alteration not only in the department's business but also in that of the accident and health industry as a whole. Up until about 1912 all insurance plans covering collections of workers had been written by insurers on the payorder arrangement, meaning that the workers themselves paid the full cost. Then, in July of 1912, one of the first true group plans went into effect when Montgomery Ward paid the entire cost of insuring its employees. A rarity at the time, Montgomery Ward's arrangement was to remain so for years. Most employers shied away from footing the bill for group plans, and as late as 1921 Metropolitan Life had in force only 69 such plans, covering 26,201 workers. Provident issued its first group policy on November 1, 1924, covering the lives of employees at the Tennessee Electric Power Company and its subsidiary, the Nashville Railway and Light Company. But given the generally unenthusiastic response of employers to group policies, Provident had concentrated on selling payorder plans, promoting them as an industrial relations tool that would cost management nothing. "Numerous employers are experiencing difficulties with their employees," ran the argument of one Provident circular in 1932, "and while in most cases the employer is doing a great deal for these employees who are giving him trouble, he would welcome any plan that would really benefit them, especially if such a plan could be put into operation without cost to him. . . . A plan will assist the employer in holding his organization together during these trying times [because] employees appreciate any evidence of human interest."

The emphasis on payorder plans came to an end during World War II, when employers were suddenly presented with two compelling economic motives to buy group policies. First, increasingly powerful labor unions were demanding additional employee benefits to compensate for the pay raises that their members had lost as a result of the wage freeze. And, second, it was becoming clear to all that the cost of group policies would soon be considered an ordinary and therefore deductible business expense for employers. As early as mid-1943, officials in the Group Department noted that "many of the cases which were closed were either on the basis of the employer paying the entire cost of the insurance program or the employer contributing substantially toward the cost." As Brooks Chandler, a rising star in the Group Department, la-

ter recalled: "The war brought about fundamental
changes in the group insurance business. Wages were
frozen and the employers were anxious to find a means
of attracting and retaining employees. Employer contributions to group insurance began to be made for
disability and medical benefits. There were tremendous opportunities to write business throughout the
country in all industries, particularly those active in
the war effort."

Gearing up for the boom in this line, the department organized its own underwriting unit, headed by
Chandler. A trim and compact man whose mind operated with the same speed and precision that characterized his every movement, Chandler brought order to
the department's hodgepodge of contracts, impression-
istic rating methods, and hit-or-miss cost accounting.
Sales executives sometimes howled and threw things
when faced with changes in the free and easy underwriting practices of old. But the reformation led by
Chandler enabled the department to handle the coming flood of business on a sound actuarial basis.

Many other insurers, reversing course, were already
preparing to invest considerable resources in the group
business, which had held little attraction for them
when it had been conducted on the payorder basis.
They would find that, in the major industries of the
Southeast, Provident enjoyed a 50-year head start on
them.

*   *   *   *   *

In the Life Department, war forced Bob Maclellan
and Sam Miles to mothball their plans for development. Early in 1942 Maclellan enlisted and was com-
missioned in the Army, with orders to report to the
financial division of the War Department. His back-

Downtown Chattanooga from Cameron Hill in the early 1890s. Landmarks are St. Paul's Episcopal Church on the right, the Chattanooga Times or Dome Building just left of center, and the old Hamilton County Courthouse at top left. The extreme top left edge marks the present site of the Provident home office complex.

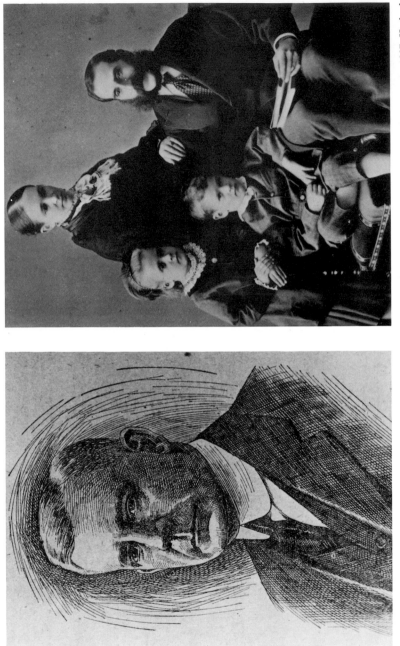

(*Left*) Reuben Harrison Hunt was one of the founders of the Mutual Medical Aid and Accident Insurance Company in 1887. He had become president in 1892, when Maclellan and McMaster bought into the company. He went on to become the architect of most of Chattanooga's important public buildings, including the Provident (now Maclellan) Building, occupied in 1924. (*Right*) Thomas Maclellan and his family in the late 1870s: wife Helen, daughter Bessie, who died before he came to Chattanooga, and son Robert Jardine, born in 1874.

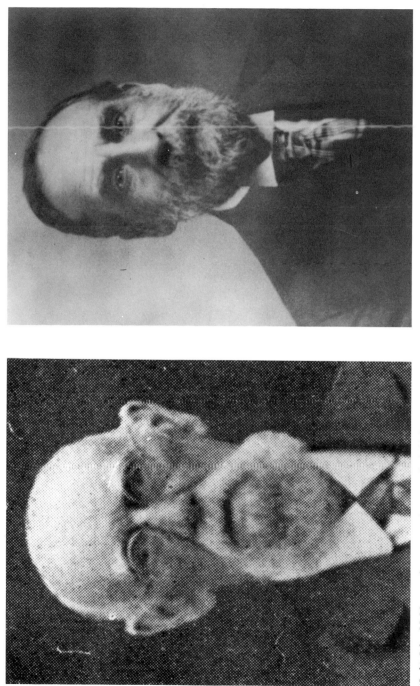

(*Left*) John McMaster, the company's original "field force," died in Philadelphia in 1930 at the age of 94. (*Right*) This photograph of Thomas Maclellan was made shortly before his accidental death in 1916.

The Most Enviable Record for Prompt
Payment of Claims.

THE PROVIDENT ACCIDENT INSURANCE COMPANY
OF CHATTANOOGA, TENN.

HAS PAID

Seven Hundred *and* Forty=Seven
..CLAIMS..

DURING THE PAST YEAR,

Amounting to $7,304.05

AND HAS PAID DURING THE PAST FEW YEARS

$25,375.11,

AND HAS NOT ONE SINGLE UNPAID JUST CLAIM.

" You have always dealt justly with our people without one single exception.
J. R. DE BARDEBLEN,
Of the Tenn Coal Iron & R R. Co."

" This Company has given satisfaction at all the Company's Plants where it has been tried.
A. S. GAINES, Superintendent,
South Pittsburg,
of the Tenn Coal Iron & R. R. Co."

A. S. GLOVER,
President.

JOHN McMASTER,
Genl. Manager.

THOS. MACLELLAN,
Sec. & Treas.

Incorporated in Tennessee.

---

819 Keystone Block,

CHATTANOOGA, TENN.

Lists of claims paid, like this one from 1895, were compiled and published for many years. Provident's principles about paying claims enabled the small company to survive in an era when most similar accident insurers did not.

RED ASH - FREE BURNING - NO CLINKER

B.R.SMITH.
 MANAGER OF SALES.   MINES AND GENERAL OFFICE   WESTERN UNION TELEGRAPH
                      LONG DISTANCE TELEPHONE

MARVEL, ALABAMA, August 15, 1914

Mr. W. C. Cartinhour, Agency Director,
 The Provident Life & Accident Insurance Co.,
  Chattanooga, Tenn.

Dear Sir:-

"ALL ORDERS, CONTRACTS AND AGREEMENTS ARE CONTINGENT UPON STRIKES, ACCIDENTS, CAR SUPPLY AND ALL OTHER DELAYS UNAVOIDABLE OR BEYOND OUR CONTROL. FREIGHT RATES ARE QUOTED FOR INFORMATION ONLY AND NOT GUARANTEED. SOUTHERN WEIGHING & INSPECTION BUREAU WEIGHTS AT MINES TO GOVERN ALL SETTLEMENTS."

   Replying to your favor of the 12th inst.
I am glad to say that I think the Blanket Plan of
insurance for our employees is far superior to the
Optionary Plan. Our men all seem to be well pleased
with your policy and the satisfactory manner in which
settlements have been made.

   It has been our experience that a large
number of miners would be classed shiftless when it
comes to providing for the future. When the earning
power of one of this class is cut off through sickness
or accident, there is nothing to support his family, and
resort must be made to subscriptions by his fellow
miners and to the Company to support them. Your form
of insurance obviates this, and we have not found a case
where it tended to keep a miner from work as soon as he
was able.   Yours very truly,

BFR/HS   President.

52

It was an article of faith at Provident that a satisfied customer is the best advertisement.
Surviving from the pre-World War I era are two small soft-cover books entitled "As Others
See Us," reproducing testimonial letters like this one from Roden Coal Company.

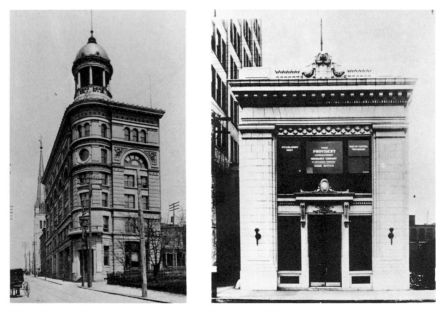

(*Top*) During its first twenty years, Provident moved frequently, occupying space in several of Chattanooga's office buildings. From 1892 until the building burned in 1897, company offices were on the fifth floor of the Richardson Building at 7th and Broad, shown here in the 1880s.

(*Bottom left*) In 1902, Provident began several years tenancy in the Chattanooga Times Building, 704 Georgia Ave.

(*Bottom right*) The company found a permanent home in 1911, moving into the James Building Annex on Broad St. This small edifice was later incorporated into the 1924 Maclellan Building.

Offices were located in the Temple Court Building from 1906 to 1910, when this photograph was made. Thomas Maclellan faces the camera; at left, standing, are Carl Cartinhour and R. J. Maclellan. Among employees in the rear are John Neligan and Miss Frances B. Amos, who became head of the Index Department. The man in the foreground is probably J. W. Kirksey.

Provident's clerical force in 1913: left to right, Miss Lindholm, Annie Light Dome, John T. Neligan, Nell Hoch Siener, Frances Amos, Miss Gould, and Bertie Amos Clift.

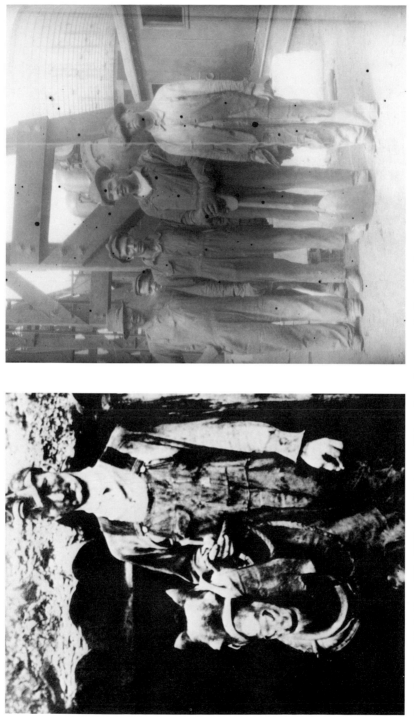

Some typical policyholders of the 1920s: a coal miner and his mule, and a group of railroad workers.

James Washington Kirksey, head of the Payorder Department, 1910–1937.

Alexander Wilds Chambliss, Provident attorney and director, in his judicial robes.

Instructions to Agents.

AGENTS of the PROVIDENT LIFE AND ACCIDENT INSURANCE COMPANY of Chattanooga are expected to acquaint themselves with the rules of the Company, and thus qualify themselves for the successful prosecution of its business.

Experience has proved that business can only be done by INTELLIGENT PERSEVERANCE. The directors require every agent to work in the Company's interest and produce good healthy business.

It is against the rules of the Company for its agents to collect any funds for the Company, unless such agent has first given sufficient bond to this Company for the security of its collections.

No charges for traveling expenses, advertising, etc., will be allowed without written permission from the head office.

Correspondence should always be to the point and brief. When writing regarding policies always give the number.

An agent should begin by taking out a policy for himself. No one can so well represent our company as one who carries a policy.

IN SOLICITING, be very careful to always state the truth and nothing but the truth. The insurance we offer is of such merit that there is no need for misrepresentation. The plain, unvarnished facts will always make our work popular. It is a mistake to talk too much. Be earnest, but give the applicant time to think and something to think about.

PERSONAL CANVASS is the keystone of success. Never delegate to another what you can do much better yourself. Avoid talking to men in groups. You will succeed better by meeting the men individually.

You will come into competition with other companies. Avoid wrangling with rival agents. Running down another com-

pany will never help yours. Have faith in and always speak well of your own company.

AGENTS SHOULD BE CLEAR IN STATING that applications sent in are always subject to the approval of the Managing Board. NO POLICY TAKES EFFECT BEFORE TWELVE O'CLOCK, NOON, OF THE DAY MENTIONED ON THE POLICY. And not then unless entrance fee and premium have been paid, or charged on the Company's books to be paid by bookkeeper or collector. In case of injury the men will have no claim unless this has been done.

It is the policy of this company to pay every just claim promptly. And in many cases technicalities will—as in the past—be waived in favor of the assured. But in all justice and fairness we expect the same prompt and honest treatment from those with whom we are dealing.

Agents should impress on bookkeepers or collectors the importance of returning our lists with the names of insured checked, immediately after pay roll is made up, that

Company secretary Thomas Maclellan issued these "Instructions to Agents" in March 1893.

The annual home office picnic was an inevitable part of summer until 1974. Four officers pose on Lookout Mountain in 1923: left to right, Marshall LeSeuer, John O. Carter, Jr., J. W. Kirksey and W. C. Cartinhour.

Families and children were part of the Provident picnics. This grouping is from 1922.

Between 1924 and 1960, the Provident Building at 721 Broad St. was both home office and symbol of vision and success.

The Provident Review

Vol. 30   Chattanooga, Tenn., November, 1929   No. 11

Wall Street Teaches a Lesson

The recent crash in Wall Street is still fresh in the public mind. Never before in history has there been anything like it.

Stock values went down like the Titanic.

An irresistible selling movement, descending upon the market with the fury of a tornado, swept the props out from under everything. The resulting debacle caught big and little alike. Small traders were wiped out and millionaires were reduced to beggary. One young woman who had been left a fortune of a million dollars lost all.

That shows what can happen to stocks.

The man who plans on leaving his widow and children a fortune of such uncertain and fluctuating value is simply kidding himself and them.

There is one sure estate that can be created — Life Insurance. The stock market may rise and fall as it will; the Bulls and the Bears can fight till they devour each other, and the ticker may tick till it wears out — the Life Insurance policy tucked away in the strong box will always be worth its full value.

Make your prospects see this in its true light and then sell them estates that will be sure and certain.

The Provident *Review* drew a moral from the stock market crash of 1929.

Salute to a Prominent Patron

OFFICIALS OF THE "BLACK EAGLE"

● In the accompanying photograph are shown prominent coal company officials. They are, left to right: Mr. Engerman, President of the Ritchie Coal Company, Chicago; Capt. John Smith, Vice-President and General Manager at Black Eagle; F. O. Sappenfield, Vice-President of the Ritchie Coal Company; J. O. Smith, President of Black Eagle, and Mr. Ritchie, Western Manager of the Pittsburgh and Ohio Coal Mining Company.

What is regarded as an unusual production record was established by the Black Eagle Smokeless Coal Company, Mullens, W. Va., by losing only three working days throughout all of 1936 and the first 11 months of 1937. The Provident appreciates the opportunity to serve this energetic organization with group welfare protection.

The only time lost, officials assert, was caused by changing to new contracts, which required two days, and a third day shutdown due to a broken pump.

The operation takes 550 tons daily from the Pocahontas seam and produces egg, stove, stoker, straight run-of-mine and slack. The coal before loading is sprayed with oil after being hand-picked in the tipple. Four grades of coal may be loaded from the tipple at one time. The oil spraying keeps down dust and reduces crumbling of the coal en route to market.

The employees of the mine live in neat bungalows along the Beckley-Mullens road in an attractive mountainous section, where they are able to raise their own garden produce. The company sponsors yearly contests to stimulate yard beautification and better gardens.

Page 22

Payorder insurance was sold through coal operators such as these, pictured in the Provident *Lookout* in January 1938.

The Claim Department in 1937. Standing, from left, Robert Bracewell, Seth Leeper and John Neligan. Seated from left, Leland Fussell, John Wesley, B. T. White, John J. Kennedy and Jerry Wilhoit. In the offices at back are F. D. Harsh, Joe T. Estes and John McDaniel, Jr.

Vice president and secretary William Carl Cartinhour in the 1930s.

Dr. Charles R. Henry was appointed Provident's first full-time medical director in 1929.

In 1937, L. N. Webb was vice president and head of the Claim and Group departments.

President R. J. Maclellan in the prime of his 50-year career.

Maclellan's two sons would also serve as Provident presidents: Hugh Owen Maclellan, Sr., left, and Robert Llewellyn Maclellan (pictured during his service in the U.S. Army during World War II).

The company celebrated its Golden Jubilee in 1937. A convention and homecoming were held in September at the Lookout Mountain Hotel, where the men at the helm posed for posterity. Left to right, H. R. Hill, assistant vice president, Group; R. L. Maclellan, vice president, Life; James Powell, agency vice president, Accident; H. C. Conley, vice president, Railroad; President R. J. Maclellan; Alexander W. Chambliss, vice president and director; W. C. Cartinhour, vice president and secretary; and L. N. Webb, vice president, Claim and Group.

Another view of the Golden Jubilee.

(*Left*) James Powell joined Provident in 1931. (*Right*) Edward L. "Billy" Mitchell signed on in 1933.

Accident Department head Jim Powell and his lieutenants in 1937. Left to right, Marshall Goodmanson, John Campbell, Powell, LaFayette Davis, and Joe Atwood.

Three consecutive heads of the Group Department steered Group through three decades of growth and change: Morgan C. "Joe" Nichols, (1943–55), center, flanked by W. Ray Webb (1955–67), left, and Billy Mitchell (1967–74) right.

Robert L. Maclellan was chief executive from 1952 to 1972.

(*Top*) Leila Kimbrough, seated, and Miss Ruth LeHardy of the payroll department welcomed a new payroll check machine in 1949. (*Bottom*) Eddie Powers and Quintell Burkeen, mainstays of the home office Building Department, in the elevator of the Maclellan Building, 1951.

Long-term anniversaries have always been occasions for celebration. At top, Railroad Department head Ray Murphy displays some gifts on his 25th company anniversary in 1949. Above, Elizabeth McDaniels receives her service pin and congratulations from L. N. Webb and Jim Powell on her 40th anniversary. She retired in 1968 after 45 years of service.

Brooks Chandler   Sam Miles, Sr.   Dudley Porter, Jr.

The fifth generation of Maclellans is represented by young Daniel Owen Maclellan, shown here in 1979 receiving Provident's millionth life insurance policy, with his father, Hugh O. Maclellan, Jr., (left) and grandfather, Hugh O. Maclellan, Sr. In the background, framed, is Provident's first life insurance policy, issued to R. J. Maclellan in 1917.

Henry C. Unruh moved from an actuarial position to be president and then chairman of the board, 1972–79.

The first building of the present Fountain Square home office complex was completed in 1960.

At top, one of Provident's most important investment properties, the 2-million-square-foot Lakewood Shopping Mall near Los Angeles, acquired in 1951. Above, the entrance to another significant property, Sarasota Square, in Sarasota, Florida.

Hugh Carey Hanlin became president in 1977 and chief executive officer in 1979.

An addition to the home office building was opened in 1972, and in January 1983, Provident expanded across Walnut Street into the new 300,000-square-foot West Building.

ground and administrative talents won him assign-
ment as head of the insurance branch of what *Nation's
Business* called the "largest insurance business ever
built": two government-operated bureaus responsible
for covering some five million military personnel and
having nearly $40 billion of life insurance in force.
One of his first tasks upon reporting for duty brought
home to him the realities not only of war but also of
life insurance marketing. A few days before the fall
of Bataan, General MacArthur's troops, besieged and
cut off by Japanese forces, were given the chance to
radio in applications for life insurance policies of up
to $10,000 each. Thirty thousand of the defenders re-
sponded, and Colonel R. C. Jenks bundled up their applications and escaped by submarine, Japanese de-
stroyers in full pursuit. After 19 days at sea, Jenks
reached Australia and immediately flew to Washington, D.C., where he handed over the bundle of insurance forms for processing by Maclellan's unit. The underwriters there got a shock when they examined the
applications. Even though MacArthur's garrison had
been within hours of doom and its defenders had faced
imminent death and injury, many of them had taken
only half the allowed insurance or even less. This curi-
ous outcome gave proof of what every insurance salesman knows, that life policies must be sold with mis-
sionary zeal. Or as the Veteran's Administration, in
its report on the incident, concluded: "apparently all
the realities of war cannot replace the insurance
agent."

Nor could anything compensate for the loss of half
of Provident's own general agents. Still, Maclellan and
Miles managed to turn the loss into a gain. Many companies severed ties with their general agents who were
called to service. Miles, on the other hand, kept the

offices of Provident's agents open and running. Besides
allowing a returning agent to go back into business
promptly, this policy instilled an intense loyalty among
the agency force, which was a boon to the department.
And even though sales had slowed, Miles was beginning to achieve higher rates of persistency, meaning
that policies, once sold, stayed sold, with no, or few
lapses. Some agents who set records for persistency
were Paul Ray, Ed Martin, W. E. Oehmig, Jr., and Wilson Reedy. Others were Grice Hunt, K. H. Hardin and
Walter Going, who opened South Carolina for the company.

War also side-lined Powell's Accident Department.
In the late 1930s Powell had begun to execute his blue-
print for change. It called for two major shifts in strategy. First, the department would gradually phase out
the sort of products that Powell had disdainfully called
"$1 policies sold in the cotton rows of the South." Such
coverages offered a policyholder scant benefits and
were tainted by association with products sold in bulk
by some companies—policies that would, in Powell's
words, "pay you a large amount if you were killed on
the dark side of the moon on a Thursday, the 14th."
Although this line of business was highly profitable,
Powell had nothing but contempt for it. Nor was he
thrilled with another characteristic of the industry:
"One of the greatest problems with the business of accident and sickness insurance was that the policies were
cancellable, and after a person had had two or three
claims, it was not uncommon to pull the rug out from
under him. Now that was bad, but that was the common practice." Common or not, Powell wanted no part
of it. Instead of offering the usual battered jalopy of
a policy, subject to recall at the drop of the hat, Powell
had begun in 1939 to write the Rolls-Royce of accident

and sickness insurance, non-cancellable coverage providing substantial benefits and guaranteed renewable
to age 65. "What we wanted was our own private little
clover patch that no one else was in," he said of the
decision. But it was not as simple as that. Powell, who
liked to tell his agents that "man's ability to kid himself
is enormous," did not kid himself about what he had
let himself in for. He might have his little clover patch,
but not before walking through a long briar patch:
"Non-can had gotten Pacific Mutual into trouble in the
1930s. But I persuaded Carl Cartinhour to do it." Once
on the hook to a policyholder there was no way of wig-
gling loose. "We learned non-can fast," said Powell.
It was a tribute to his growing stature in the industry
that in 1939 the Health and Accident Underwriters
Conference had elected him its president. At 37, Powell
was the youngest man to have held that office.

The non-cancellable coverage developed slowly, for
Powell chose not to seek corporate funds for this risky
venture, but rather to finance it out of earnings set
aside from his department's standard monthly and
commercial lines. These lines attracted a diverse assortment of customers: major-league baseball umpires,
volunteer fire departments, teachers' groups, doctors,
lawyers, dentists, students at Chattanooga's private
schools, and the 30,000-member American Automobile
Association. There were certain groups, though, that
the department judged it could not afford to insure.
Twice it turned down applications made by the Ring-
ling Bros. and Barnum & Bailey Circus.

Powell's second strategic initiative had been to take
the department's products out of the hands of casualty
brokers, who knew little about insuring people, and
place those products with accident and sickness brokerage firms which, like the Tom Hopkins Agency in

Pittsburgh and the McNeill Agency in Boston, had the specialized knowledge and network of contacts required to sell Provident's coverage aggressively. But no sooner had these two changes begun than the war robbed Powell of the manpower with which to carry them through.

Not war but time caused the departure of one leader, who had been the first to carry Provident's coverage from coast to coast. In January of 1941, after 15 years as chief of the Railroad Department, Harry Conley retired. As his successor, the board chose Raymond R. Murphy, agency manager and Conley's right hand since 1926. The son of a shoemaker, Murphy cut a dashing figure and had the brains and know-how to match. By the end of 1941 Murphy, together with his principal assistant, David N. Parks, pushed Railroad's income up by ten percent, to $1.7 million. Dry and lifeless figures these, but Parks translated them into human terms: "A train traveling at 50 miles an hour, day and night and with no stops, would require more than four months to go over the main-line tracks of the railroads whose employees are served by Provident's Railroad Department. The total main-line mileage of the more than 140 different railroads would reach six times around the earth at the equator." One of the railroads, the Chesapeake and Ohio, alone had 17,000 employees covered by Provident.

Another promotion of consequence occurred in January of 1943 when Joe Nichols, to the delight of almost everybody, was officially named head of the Group Department. He had been chief of the department in all but name since 1940, but not until the nominal head, Howard Hill, retired was the title formally bestowed on Nichols. As his second-in-command, Nichols chose W. Ray Webb, who had joined the company in 1924 and specialized in coal matters with such success that he had received the hard-won respect of agents in the coalfields, as well as the unofficial title "coal guru." Rising fast, too, was the more junior Billy Mitchell, whom Nichols brought into the home office as an assistant.

By the end of 1945 John Campbell, Bill Rader, Bob Maclellan and others who had answered the call to arms were returning to pick up where they had left off. Out of the 52 men and women who had gone into service, there was a single casualty: Lieutenant Charles H. Campbell, navigator of a Flying Fortress, shot down over Austria on his 46th mission, a bombing raid out of Italy. John Saint survived the African invasion and landings in Sicily, Anzio and Southern France to come back unscathed to the Accident Department.

With the dislocations of war at an end, Provident's operations began to produce impressive gains. At the end of 1946, total premiums collected by the health and accident industry stood at $665 million, or 15 percent above the year before. Provident, by contrast, increased its accident and health income by $3.2 million, a 25 percent gain and nearly double the national average. Provident's assets were up by more than $5 million, to $37.2 million, and, for the first time since the onset of the Depression, no bonds were in default and no mortgage loans in arrears. Growing fast from a strong financial base, Provident was poised to capitalize on the post-war boom.

7

Walnut Street Hill

IN THE FALL of 1947, R. J. Maclellan, acting with his usual reserve and canny patience, embarked on a project whose existence would remain a secret to all but four other Provident executives. Not so secret was the problem Maclellan intended to solve. Provident was running out of room. More than 500 employees jostled for elbow room in the home office on Broad Street. To relieve the congestion, management considered buying and building on the only available piece of property adjacent to the home office. But as Maclellan knew, the plan would offer only a temporary solution at best. With Provident's work force and business increasing at the rate of 15 percent yearly, the company would soon outgrow the proposed building and be left without paths of expansion in any direction. When that happened, management would face the prospect of splitting operations among several buildings scattered around town. For Maclellan, who assiduously cultivated a sense of family togetherness within the organization, any such fragmentation was unthinkable. To stay intact, the rapidly expanding company would have to relocate on a tract of land large enough to meet its space requirements for decades.

After studying a number of sites, some suburban and one—the northwest block at the intersection of Ninth

and Chestnut, which another insurer would later oc-
cupy—Maclellan set his sights on the area directly
across from the Hamilton County Courthouse, known
as Walnut Street Hill. A trace of sentiment entered into
his calculations, for it was at 518 Walnut Street that
Thomas Maclellan had lived and Robert J. Maclellan
had enjoyed his young manhood. That Provident's new
office would rise atop the site of his family home was
a source of delight to Maclellan as well as to his sons
Bob and Hugh, who together with Cartinhour and Les
Webb formed the exclusive group working on the project. Then, too, Walnut Street Hill, a decaying residential section, was one of the few areas downtown where
Maclellan might acquire a sizable tract at a favorable
price. But the acquisition posed a logistical nightmare.
More than 50 separate plots would have to be bought
up, one at a time, slowly and quietly, without showing
Provident's hand in the transactions. If either by word
or by deed Maclellan revealed his design, property
values on Walnut Street Hill would skyrocket beyond
Provident's reach.

Maclellan saw no reason to inform the board of his
plan or to draw on corporate funds to finance it. Im-
mensely wealthy now, he put up $171,000 of his own
money for starters. By the end of 1949 he held title to
seven parcels of land. Then, in 1950, the plan for Walnut Street Hill was delayed when war broke out in
Korea. War-time demands suddenly made building
materials scarce, and no one could predict when the
supply would return to normal. Faced with this uncertainty, Provident's executives went back to their earlier
and more modest plan of erecting an annex to the home
office on Broad Street. Completed in 1951, the five-story
annex, known as the West Building, took care of the
company's immediate need for space. Looking ahead,

however, the executives continued acquiring land on Walnut Street Hill.

To handle the transactions, Maclellan chose his son Hugh Owen, a quiet and gentle man who shunned the limelight as resolutely as had his grandfather Thomas. Upon graduating from Cornell University in 1935, Hugh had joined Provident, specializing in investment policy. By temperament and training, the unassuming, financially astute Maclellan was well suited to carry out the sensitive mission entrusted him. Operating through a host of agents and sub-agents, he gradually bought up Walnut Street Hill, all the while concealing Provident's ultimate objective from employees and realtors. Only in a closely held company like Provident, where one family controlled more than half the stock and where budgets never circulated and internal auditors were unknown, could so massive a project have been kept secret until completed ten years later.

While these moves went unnoticed, changes in the company's leadership were plain to see. Many of the officers who remembered the half-nickel-a-day policy passed from the scene. Judge Alexander Wilds Chambliss, chief architect of Provident's conversion in 1910 to a stock company, had suffered a fatal stroke on September 30, 1947, at the age of 83. His long-standing connection with Provident, dating from 1895, was maintained by a son, John A. Chambliss, and a grandson, Jac Chambliss, who served as directors and legal advisers. But the man destined to become counselor to the inner circle of top management was Dudley Porter, Jr., an urbane and patrician young lawyer who spoke in the mellifluous tones of the Virginia tidewater. Joining Provident in 1949, Porter would become one of Bob Maclellan's closest confidants, valued for his combination of legal knowledge, political finesse and strategic judgment.

In 1951 Porter organized the company's first subsidiary, Provident Life and Casualty Insurance Company. The name was something of a misnomer, since Provident Life and Casualty sold no casualty insurance. Instead, it existed to enable its parent to do business properly in New York within that state's insurance laws, which required a company licensed there to abide by New York's regulations not only in New York but also everywhere else it did business. The incorporation of Provident Life and Casualty was complicated, however, by an antiquated Tennessee law prohibiting one insurance company from owning more than five percent of another's stock. Originally enacted as a safeguard against hostile takeovers, the law had the unintended effect of preventing a Tennessee company from organizing its own subsidiary. Porter began calling on state lawmakers, explaining the problem with all the sweet reasonableness at his command. "Dudley is a master diplomat," said one who had seen him in action. "He has the patience to sit outside a congressman's office for five hours in order to get to see him. His natural courtesy and low-key approach are captivating, and he cannot be refused." And he was not. In the summer of 1951, the Tennessee legislature made the necessary amendment, and on October 17 Provident entered New York, the one major market that had remained beyond reach. Premiums now flowed in from 46 states, the District of Columbia, and Canada, which Provident had entered in 1948.

Besides Judge Chambliss, other departing executives included Dr. Charles Henry, retiring after 22 years and succeeded by Dr. William R. Bishop; Keith Kropp, head of Claims, who died suddenly and was replaced by J. Robert Bracewell; and treasurer J. O. Carter, Jr., who retired in 1955 at the end of a 38-year career during which he had seen the assets under his care grow from $340,000 to $101 million. Hugh Maclellan then acquired the duties of treasurer and head of the Investment Department.

Of all the managerial changes, perhaps the most significant occurred when Carl Cartinhour retired at the end of March 1951, at age 62. Cartinhour could rightfully claim as much credit as any other executive for Provident's explosive growth since 1916. Much of this growth was directly attributable to the two acquisitions in which Cartinhour had played major roles: the Standard Accident Company in 1926 and the Southern Surety Company in 1931.

Planning for his own retirement, R. J. Maclellan in October 1947 had issued a directive outlining a new chain of command in which all production departments reported to Bob Maclellan. Less than a year after Cartinhour's retirement, on January 30, 1952, Bob was named president and R. J. assumed the newly created office of chairman of the board.

Bright, intense and energetic, Bob gradually took on much of the responsibility formerly shared by his father, Cartinhour and Webb. Like his father, Bob emphasized three corporate values: scrupulous integrity in all things, the concept of the work force as a family unit, and fiscal restraint. But Bob's approach to management differed markedly from that of his father. Whereas the elder Maclellan had delegated considerable responsibility to Cartinhour, Webb and others throughout the company, Bob preferred to deal himself with a large volume of details. His encyclopedic knowledge of happenings large and small in all departments amazed his subordinates and worried his friends, who knew of the grueling schedule he maintained to master and manage so much material. Nor did Bob cast himself so completely in the paternal role characteristic of his father. When officers performed below his expectations, he expressed his displeasure in forceful language.

As always, though, each of the four production departments operated as a semi-autonomous unit, having its own policies, procedures and cherished traditions. Department heads functioned as barons, accountable solely to Bob Maclellan. As Hollywood-handsome Jim Powell later explained, hammering the desk for emphasis: "I was in charge of the whole damn ball of wax. Completely. I had the final authority on rates, on everything in the [Accident Department] except investments. And anything that went wrong came off my fanny and nobody else's."

Powell's backside, despite the daring venture into non-cancellable coverage, remained unscathed, though the quaking secretaries and staffers exposed to his withering sarcasm and profane outbursts must have concluded that the boss was being flayed alive. "We'd tell our wives how mean Jim was to us," laughed one victim of Powell's whiplash tongue, "but they wouldn't believe us because when he met them at parties he'd turn on the charm." Said another insider: "Jim had three standard closings to his letters. The first was 'Sincerely,' which meant that he had cut you to ribbons in the letter. The second was 'Cordially,' which meant that you had done a mediocre job. The last was 'Fondly,' which meant he was pleased with you. You didn't even have to read the letter to find out where you stood. All you had to do was look at the closing." Powell's frankness, combined with his style and brains, alienated some, but inspired fierce loyalty in others. "He was like a father to me," averred James Sedgwick, Powell's administrative assistant. Eston Whelchel, thinking out loud about the peculiar mixture of rancor and respect that Powell elicited, observed: "I probably quit as many times as any other branch office manager. But to this day, when a problem comes up, I sometimes ask myself, 'Now, how would Jim Powell handle this?' " It was Jack Spinner, manager of the Philadelphia office, who came closest to expressing the feelings Powell aroused. During a training session that Spinner attended, each student was asked to introduce himself and describe his work. When Spinner's turn came, he gave his name and said: "I work for Jim Powell. He's an irascible, egocentric son of a bitch, and I would follow him into hell." Powell would have liked that.

His marching orders sent Spinner, Whelchel and the others into regions where Provident was not exactly a familiar name. They found that the name carried little weight with insurance brokers in places such as San Francisco, Los Angeles, Chicago and Newark. Some brokers were openly scornful of a little-known company located in Chattanooga, a city they assumed to be populated exclusively with hillbillies and hound dogs. "Does the president of Provident wear shoes?" asked one doubter when Marshall Goodmanson called for an appointment.

A tenacious lot, these branch managers survived their first lean years and in time began to win major accounts that eased the way to additional business. Goodmanson sold coverage to the 1,500-member San Francisco Medical Society, a pivotal account that earned him wider acceptance among the area's brokers. In Chicago, John Campbell scored a similar breakthrough with the Wisconsin Medical Society, an account brokered through Charles O. Finley, who would later achieve recognition as the colorful owner of the Oakland Athletics.

Galled by the fact that Provident's name was largely unknown outside the Southeast, Powell decided to advertise in five national magazines: *Business Week, Newsweek, The Saturday Evening Post, Time* and *U.S. News and World Report.* Through these media Powell promoted his Salary Continuance Plan, designed to protect top executives against loss of salary in case of disability. The advertisements pictured a vacant desk and a solemn group of directors sitting around a boardroom table. One asked bluntly, "How long can we continue to pay John while he is disabled?" Many companies got the message. The first plan covered 450 executives at the Ford Motor Company.

Another program that promised to add thousands of policyholders and millions in premium dollars was underway in the Railroad Department. Under the leadership of Ray Murphy, the department joined with other insurers to develop a nationwide hospital-and-surgical program covering some 500,000 non-operating members of the railroad brotherhoods. Provident was one of 12 companies selected by a committee of management and labor to underwrite the coverage, and its share of the total premiums was expected to exceed $5 million a year. Effective March 1, 1955, the agreement was then the largest single group hospital-and-surgical policy ever written.

*   *   *   *   *

The company's big moneymaker, Joe Nichols' Group Department, outdid itself in 1954. That summer Nichols and Ray Webb reached an agreement with the Federal Civil Service Commission, which awarded

Provident a $135-million share of the group life program put into effect on two million civil servants. Of the 250 companies writing group life, Provident now ranked 11th, as measured by coverage in force. Later that same year the department achieved a breakthrough when it won the Campbell Soup Company account, which represented the first Provident client with coast to coast facilities. To Billy Mitchell went the credit for hatching the deal.

Over the years Mitchell had built a seemingly endless network of friends in high places. Among them was an executive of the venerable insurance brokerage firm of Johnson and Higgins, which, as it happened, had been retained by Campbell Soup to solicit bids from insurers and recommend which to accept. While Mitchell worked to persuade Johnson and Higgins that Provident offered the best buy, Brooks Chandler spent two weeks in a stuffy Philadelphia hotel room, poring over a confusing array of insurance contracts in force at dozens of Campbell's plants. Benefits, rates and contractual language varied enormously from plant to plant, owing to the vagaries of collective bargaining. Chandler's task was to write an acceptable master contract, eliminating the variances. Although neither an actuary nor a lawyer by training, Chandler possessed a keen and retentive mind that had enabled him to acquire the more useful skills of both professions. Said one colleague, "Brooks was more of an actuary than most certified actuaries."

True to form, Chandler produced a contract that won favor with Johnson and Higgins, as had Billy Mitchell's ingratiating ways. The brokerage house recommended Provident and Campbell's accepted. With 18,000 U.S. employees, Campbell's would add another digit to the department's bottom line. Better still, having the account made it easier to get others like it, much as money begets money. The account also marked the beginning of a long and mutually profitable relationship between Provident and Johnson and Higgins. Recognizing the part Mitchell had played in bringing this about, his friends at the brokerage house later presented him with an ornate and whimsically worded plaque entitled "A Salute to the Provident Life and Billy Mitchell Insurance Company."

Joe Nichols, celebrating his 25th anniversary with Provident in May of 1955, had every reason to congratulate himself on a job well done. As an associate of his observed with considerable justice: "Kirksey gave birth to the Group Department, and Joe Nichols raised it." Nichols had indeed guided the department through a period of awkward transitions, as it changed from a payorder business to a true group business, from flat rates to guaranteed retentions, from specializing in covering a few industries to handling the needs of a diverse assortment of industries. A sampling of its varied clients included Stonega Coal and Coke, Burlington Mills, the Greenbrier, Oertel Brewing, Wheeling Steel, Hagerstown Teamsters' Welfare Fund, Duke Power, International Paper and the University of Wisconsin.

Taking note of Nichols' performance, the board had elected him a director. He could look forward to another 15 years of increasing influence within the company. His success was evident. But Joe Nichols was not content. For some time, as he afterwards recalled, he had "wanted to get into some kind of work where there was no personal ambition involved at all." His conviction grew that his true calling was in the ministry of the Episcopal Church. On several occasions he had mentioned this conviction to the Maclellans, father and son. So far as he could ever tell, neither of them quite believed he was serious.

But he was. On his birthday, October 19, in 1955, Nichols resigned, exchanging his princely salary at Provident for the comparatively meager living of an Episcopal priest-in-the-making. R. J. and Hugh Maclellan signed a resolution of the executive committee, which reluctantly accepted Nichols' resignation. On the day it took effect, October 31, the executive committee met again. Its decision: "Since Mr. Nichols' desire is for full-time church work, the Committee voted to continue his salary for six months, and at the expiration of this time, to assist him in his efforts in his chosen field." For his own part, Nichols moved on in his new work, never looking back.

His departure set in motion an upward bubbling of executives in the Group Department. Ray Webb moved up to head the department; assisting him were Billy Mitchell as vice president, and Brooks Chandler as assistant vice president and secretary.

Meanwhile, the acquisition of Walnut Street Hill proceeded smoothly, if slowly. A widow who had lived there all her 73 years refused to sell unless granted a leasehold for the balance of her days. It was granted. While Hugh Maclellan worked the jigsaw puzzle of real estate transactions that would alleviate Provident's growing pains, another group of executives put their minds to a problem natural to a company growing at the compound rate of 20 percent a year: processing Everests of paperwork.

On the recommendation of chief actuary Henry Unruh, whose influence was on the rise, the executive committee named a group of five to study and advise on the feasibility of introducing a new generation of machines, known around the company as "electronic brains." The Electronic Data Processing Committee, as the team was called, was composed of comptroller Glenn Johnson, tabulating equipment supervisor Victor Covey, operations officer Kenneth Piper, planner Abner Boyd, and Unruh, who served as chairman. Although many businessmen still regarded computers as little more than interesting toys (only in 1954 was the first computer installed in a private business), Unruh and his team needed only three months to convince Bob Maclellan that Provident must have one of these thinking machines. On July 12, 1955, Maclellan made the announcement: "As you probably know from magazine and news accounts, machines are now available which will analyze records, make calculations, and produce statistical reports at fantastic speeds. It is a pleasure to tell you that the Provident has ordered one of these 'electronic brains.' The machine, called the IBM Magnetic Drum Calculator, is the first of its type to be ordered in the Chattanooga area. The computer can memorize 20,000 digits of information, which are accessible in less than 3/1000ths of a second. The machine can make 2,000 additions or subtractions per second, 60 multiplications per second, and 50 divisions per second. Instructions for handling the data or for solving a problem are stored in one section of the machine's 'memory.' When the machine is started the results are produced automatically."

But before the IBM-650, which arrived in November of 1956, would perform such marvels, it had first to be housebroken. To design the programs that would tell it how to behave, Unruh selected five young men: Don Arthur, Tom Collum, Frank Klaasse, Bob Martin and Rhea Watkins. Because programming was still in its infancy, these men had to rely largely on their own ingenuity. For months on end they put in a succession of 14-hour days, tinkering, improvising and slowly

taming the machine by trial and error. Working closely
with them were Tom Stimson, Clarence Gay, Latta
Johnston, Jerry Dean and Bill Bishop, who were responsible for finding the smoothest ways to computerize the manual operations of the various departments.

As head of the EDP teams, Henry Unruh dealt not
only with the technical side of the conversion but also
with its political ramifications. To varying degrees,
three of the vice presidents in charge of production
departments saw computerization as a threat to their
administrative independence. All strongly sales-
minded, they were less than enthusiastic about having
outside technicians underfoot, delving through depart-
mental records and disrupting established procedures.
Each was a forceful personality, easily capable of in-
timidating officers their junior, as Unruh was.

But Unruh was not easily intimidated. At 42, he had
seen more of the world than most men twice his age.
Born near Hamburg, Germany, the child of Mennonite
Dutch-German missionaries originally from the Cri-
mea, Unruh grew up in India, and by the age of 16
had sailed around the world twice. Although English
was his third language, after German and an Indian
dialect, no trace of a German accent remained. His
paternal grandparents had lost their nationality during
the Russian Revolution. For years thereafter, Unruh
and his family endured the hardships visited upon
stateless persons. It was not until 1946 that Henry, by
then a naturalized Canadian citizen, gained permission to settle in the United States. Because of his place
of birth, he had to enter the country under the quota
for German immigrants, which, to his surprise, was
not filled at the time. He immediately placed an "actuary available" advertisement in the *National Under-*

writer. He received six responses, replied to the one from Provident and on April 1 joined the company.

A stranger in strange lands for much of his life, Unruh was tough-minded, yet flexible. He violated the stereotype of the actuary as absent-minded professor lost in a cloud of abstractions. "The pragmatic actuary," some dubbed him. It was a high compliment, considering that most of the company thought a pragmatic actuary to be a contradiction in terms. He also took a decidedly wry and irreverent approach to life, a trait that he demonstrated some years later in an exchange with Bob Maclellan. Maclellan, who awarded service pins with all the solemnity of a general bestowing medals on his troops, noticed one day that Unruh's lapel was bare.

"Henry," he ever so politely inquired, "where is your service pin?"

"Well, Bob," Unruh answered, "I guess I must have left it on my pajamas."

Not easily awed or diverted from his purpose, Unruh kept the conversion to computer running smoothly, though he sometimes encountered fierce resistance. "We'd tear each other's eyes out at ten o'clock in the morning," said Unruh of his battle of wills with one department head, "but by four o'clock there was no grudge held by anybody." Much later, after he retired, that same department head would point with pride to the department's computerized processing of applications.

The pragmatic actuary was also making his presence felt in the Life Department, where he showed a flair for designing products that quickly caught on with agents and customers. The first of these was called the Programmed Income Plan. Brought out in 1947, it was the department's best-selling policy from 1948 to 1952. Another hit came in 1954 when Unruh, working with Sam Miles and agency manager Ed Jones, designed a novel and, at the time, risky policy; its $20,000 minimum size and first year cash value made it unique among whole life products then being offered by the nation's life insurance companies. Some analysts considered the rapid cash buildup unsound, but the policy was an instant success with consumers. Together with an insured pension plan called Pension Trust Life, this policy accounted for some 65 percent of the department's sales over the next six years. General agents armed with these products put business on the books as never before. Ed Martin, of the Chattanooga agency, had a particularly rewarding experience in 1954. On a single day Martin sold $1 million worth of pension trust to the Chattanooga Medicine Company, in an arrangement he had worked out with his friend Lupton Patten, president of the patent-medicine company and a recent addition to Provident's board.

The driving force behind pension trust was William W. Voigt. According to many of his associates, if anyone ever had it all, that person was Bill Voigt. Independently wealthy, recipient of a Harvard M.B.A., a confidant of Bob Maclellan, Voigt was a ruggedly handsome and charming man whose wide-ranging intellect dazzled even the down-to-earth Unruh. "Bill was the kind of guy who didn't care whether he had a contract or not to issue; all he cared about was getting a piece of business sold and then coming home and writing the contract," said Unruh. "I found him to be a natural actuary, able to do complicated mathematical problems in his head where we actuaries had to scratch it out on paper. He was a salesman, innovator, actuary—everything in one person."

Starting out in 1948 with a staff of one secretary, Voigt had built Provident's insurance pension business from nothing to $2 million in 1954. Assisted by G. N. Dickinson, Jr. and John K. Witherspoon, Jr., Voigt increased the amount to $5 million in 1955. That same year, when the chief of the department, Sam Miles, moved up to secretary of the company, Voigt effectively assumed command of the Life Department, though he would share authority with agency manager Ed Jones.

*   *   *   *   *

The year 1955 was a golden year for Robert J. Maclellan, who celebrated his 50th anniversary with Provident. On September 15, 700 employees gathered at Chattanooga's palatial Tivoli Theatre for a ceremony in his honor. There his daughter, Mrs. Walter Hoyle, unveiled a life-size bronze bust of Maclellan, created by Miss Belle Kenney, a New York sculptress. Son Bob pinned on his father's lapel the first 50-year pin in the company's history, and son Hugh presented a Golden Anniversary Scroll signed by each officer of the company and each member of the board. In a 50-day sales drive, agents had collected 50,000 applications for all kinds of insurance and sent each application, along with an anniversary greeting from the salesman, to Maclellan. The home office presented him a silver serving piece, fashioned in London during the reign of George I.

There was also the fond tribute paid him by an old friend, Leslie Webb. Maclellan's unshakable integrity, Webb told the assembly, was woven into the pattern of Provident's success. "When he came to the company he did everything, training agents, keeping books, getting payroll contracts with coal and lumber companies," said Webb. "When he started, the company had an income of about $2,500 a month from all sources. Now, in his 50th year, it is collecting more than $5 million a month."

Maclellan responded with words typical of a man so polite, so considerate, so outwardly unimpressed by the fact that he was a millionaire many times over. "You give me much credit," he said. "But the greatest share of the credit for the Provident as it stands today, and for what it will be in the future, belongs to many men and women. These have been a happy 50 years. I was sold on the Provident and the insurance business when I first joined the company 50 years ago. From the beginning our fundamental philosophy has been that the interests of the policyholder come first. That philosophy has been the primary force in making the Provident the great institution it is today. You people, and others like you through the years, have helped to make it so."

Although no one realized it at the time, Maclellan had delivered his farewell address to Provident. In the early morning hours of June 7, 1956, while dressing for work, Maclellan died of heart failure, as quietly and to all appearances as peacefully as he had lived. There were many tributes to him, from his pastor's eulogy to editorials in local newspapers. Of them all, the memorial by Leslie Webb stands as the best characterization of a man whose impenetrable reserve had made him a shadowy presence to many. It reads in part: "All of us have lost a true friend in the passing of Mr. Robert J. Maclellan. . . . A quiet sense of humor, modesty and humility, a complete honesty, a desire to be a friend to everyone; these were the trademarks of his personality, and they never changed throughout his life. . . . His most enjoyable occasions with the

Provident were such gatherings as Company field conventions and meetings, the Home Office Christmas lunch, and annual picnics. The Provident's valued institutional integrity . . . can be attributed in large part to Mr. Maclellan's leadership and his association with us as individuals. His primary influence was through the example he set as a man and as a Christian gentleman rather than by the directions from a chief executive. The insurance business is a better place to work because of his having been a part of it. His community is a better place to live because of his having lived here. Many of us at the Provident and in the Chattanooga area had known him for many years. Many others had never met him. But I know from personal experience that all of us have lost a true friend."

Maclellan's works lived on, however. In his will he had created the Maclellan Foundation, endowing it with a considerable block of his Provident stock. To Provident itself he left a bequest of inestimable value: Walnut Street Hill. In July of 1957, nearly ten years after Maclellan had moved to acquire this area, Provident owned 16 acres there. Bob Maclellan formed a building committee composed of himself, his brother Hugh, Leslie Webb, Sam Miles and Kenneth Piper. Like their predecessors who planned the 1924 building, these officers involved themselves in the smallest details of design and construction. From May of 1957 to October of 1960, they held 270 recorded meetings.

Upon the recommendation of the consulting firm of Ebasco and Associates, the building committee approved a design submitted by New York architects Otto Egger and Dan Higgins. It called for a seven-story structure occupying half the block directly north of the Hamilton County Courthouse. On November 17 a crowd of 900 faithful gathered at the construction site to watch Bob Maclellan climb into the cab of a huge power shovel and push a lever. An iron arm groaned and clanked and a steel-toothed bucket picked up the first shovelful of dirt. As Maclellan climbed down to the cheers of his audience, workers of the Turner Construction Company took over, removing the first of many thousands of cubic yards of earth in order to lower the hill 17½ feet.

By early December, the power shovels had disappeared, and in their place pile drivers banged steel beams down around a red clay hole, 20 feet deep, that would form the basement of the seven-story, $7 million building. The building committee had discussed at length the question of what material should be used for the outer walls. On visits to Manhattan, Webb and Piper inspected granite buildings, concluding that granite took on a greasy stain as it aged. Limestone, they discovered, tended to show grime in unpredictable patterns in parts of the Rockefeller Center. Marble, hard, shiny and durable, weathered best of all, they concluded. The committee's decision to use marble, despite its high price tag, was influenced by their plan to extend the building to the end of the block in the years ahead. With its excellent weathering characteristics, marble would allow the future addition to be almost indistinguishable from the original building.

The steel frame rose fast, topping out on April 23, 1959. In July the walls of white Georgia marble began to take shape, and by December the edifice, its shell complete, stood high above downtown Chattanooga. Over the Labor Day weekend of 1960, Provident's 800 home office employees moved into the new building. The white marble structure, 242 feet long and 138 feet wide, looked down on a landscaped plaza of fountains and flora, including azalea, virburnum, dogwood, hemlock and locust. It was the largest office building in Chattanooga and the only one with its own front yard.

This new addition to Chattanooga's skyline opened with a series of festivities culminating on December 7, when employees and their families and friends attended a dedication ceremony. Afterwards, the company settled down to business again, though streams of visitors still came to have lunch in the cafeteria located on the seventh floor, or to walk through the lobby, faced with teak and trimmed with dark grey and dark green marble from the Italian Alps, Southern France and Vermont. Just inside the front entrance stood the bronze bust of Robert J. Maclellan, whose name the former home office building now bore.

Even for those who did not climb the hill to visit, Provident could not be ignored. All that Christmas, a giant 30-foot Christmas tree, marked by a flashing star and 300 colored lights, stood in the plaza. It was visible for miles, a variation of the old Scandinavian custom of putting a tree on top of a building in thanks to the neighbors who had helped construct it.

8

"A Quiet Giant"

PROVIDENT EMERGED from the 1950s with a momentum propelling it beyond its small-town origins. Looking back on the decade, Henry Unruh described it as a "period of rapid growth which removed Provident from the classification of a small regional company and established it as a force to be reckoned with on a national scale." The company had seen other periods of breakaway growth, but none to compare with the 1950s. At the end of 1949, after 62 years of business, Provident was collecting $32.2 million in premiums. But between 1950 and 1959, annual premium collections swelled to $107.7 million, an increase of $75.4 million for the decade and more than double the gains made during the previous 62 years. Measured by insurance in force, Provident ranked 35th in size among the then more than 1,200 life insurance companies in the United States and Canada.

The stellar performance of the 1950s was a hard act to follow, yet the bountiful gains of the 1960s stole the show. After a slump in 1958, the American economy took off on the longest sustained recovery in the nation's history. Wages, retail sales, construction and industrial output climbed steadily upward while inflation inched along at 1.7 percent a year. Riding high on this floodtide of prosperity, Provident nearly doubled its business in the six years between 1959 and

1965, when premium income shot up from $107.7 million to $210.7 million. Assets multiplied apace. In his report to the stockholders in 1966, Bob Maclellan took note of this exponential growth: "The first $100 million of assets was reached on December 31, 1954; the $200 million mark on June 30, 1960, five years and six months later; the third $100 million on December 31, 1963, three years and six months later; with the $400 million milestone being attained in two years and nine months."

This growth in assets had been fueled largely by a boom in the sale of individual life products, which, being relatively long-term liabilities, built up the company's cash reserves faster than did individual accident and health or group products. Historically, life insurance had been a slow-growing part of Provident's business, amounting in 1952 to only $1 billion in force. But its development quickened noticeably in the late 1950s, and by 1964 life insurance in force totaled $5 billion. Some 70 percent of that amount had been written through the Group Department, through plans covering employees of companies scattered across the nation. The remaining 30 percent was generated by the Life Department itself, which had begun to show signs of vigor.

Known in its early years as an anemic performer, the department had responded to the careful ministrations of Sam Miles, Bill Voigt and Henry Unruh. Following the lead set by Miles in 1935, the department had gradually moved into a higher income market. Miles' idea was to hire "quality men to produce quality business." To help him carry out his idea, Miles depended primarily on Voigt and Unruh. Voigt's personal magnetism drew high-powered agents to Provident, while Unruh's inventive mind designed the products that kept them there. Their efforts had moved the department into a more affluent and profitable market, as reflected by the steady rise in the average size of individual policies sold: $6,212 in 1952, $16,887 in 1962, and $32,609 in 1966.

If any one factor lay behind this success, it was the executives' ability to recruit and retain exceptional agents. The pivotal role of the agent stemmed from the fact that the typical consumer bought a life insurance policy on an agent's recommendation, rather than on the actual merits of the policy. Insurance rates varied widely, and, even though a policy might be the best of its kind on the market, it stood little chance of catching the consumer's eye unless promoted aggressively by agents.

Those in the department who had excelled in the cultivation of agents included Miles, Voigt, and until his death in 1960, Ed Jones. They offered the successful agent one inducement that he would have been hard-pressed to find elsewhere, independence. Most life insurers maintained captive agency forces, ruled and regulated by the home office. Provident, on the other hand, developed a more decentralized setup. Known in the trade as the Personal Producing General Agent system, or PPGA, this approach allowed an agent to be his own boss. As described by a veteran of the Life Department, this meant that the department "provided an agent with products and some services and issued policies, but we didn't tell agents how they should sell or lead them to business or pay them except for business produced." The Life Department provided general agents the opportunity to run their offices as they saw fit, without home office intervention.

The PPGA system appealed to successful agents who had grown restive under close supervision elsewhere.

In fact, many of them jumped ship, signing on with Provident. They were also attracted by the Life Department's open-handed attitude toward compensation. Commissions were liberal, cruises to exotic locations were frequent, and there was membership in the Continental Club. Brainchild of Bill Voigt, the Continental Club rewarded top agents with luxury automobiles. By maintaining high sales, an agent could win a new Lincoln or Cadillac every two years.

The department took good care of its agents, and they in turn produced a flood of new business. That fact was apparent in 1967 when 113 Provident agents held membership in the Million Dollar Round Table, a larger contingent than that of any other investor-owned U.S. life insurance company. Among these were seven agents who, according to Sam Miles, had consistently ranked among the department's top producers since the mid-1940s: Bill Brakebill, Floyd Dupree, Joe Hanks, Ken Hardin, Grice Hunt, Ed Martin and DeForest Spencer. A Chattanooga-based agent, Spencer earned the distinction of having produced at least one application a week, month after month, since first joining Provident in the late 1930s. Following in his father's footsteps, agent Richard W. Spencer had produced an application a week since 1955.

No matter how fast the business poured in, however, Provident's service departments continued the policy of fair and prompt dealing laid down in leaner times by Thomas Maclellan and John McMaster. Snafus were rare, particularly in Robert Bracewell's Claims Department. Evidence that Provident had made the transition from a small to a large company without growing inattentive to individual policyholders came at the end of 1965 when, after having paid some 4,000 claims each working day of the year, or one every six seconds, Bracewell reported that only 23 policyholders had seen fit to sue Provident over its handling of their claims. And from a few conscience-stricken claimants Bracewell received envelopes without return addresses, containing unsigned apologies and money as atonement for having collected on false claims. One woman in Denver, who signed herself "a troubled client," sent $121 on the advice of her confessor.

Others, though, could hardly conceal their glee at having put one over on the insurance company. There was the doctor in North Carolina who, in the words of one agent, "took out tonsils by the bucketfuls and sent us bills by the truckload." The doctor made no secret of his intention to remove every set of tonsils that came his way. "I've got the sweetest deal," he would tell casual acquaintances. "I get $10 for each pair of tonsils I take out, and every kid here has 'em."

Little could be done to curb his enthusiasm, short of petitioning the appropriate medical association to take disciplinary action against him, a course that the Claims Department judged to be impractical almost to the point of impossibility. Although cases of this sort were a persistent source of frustration around the department, claimsmen nonetheless derived satisfaction from detecting and thwarting a variety of fraudulent schemes. The work could be gritty, but it also offered the kind of intrigue not ordinarily associated with insurance companies. For in a business where people routinely deal with life and death at a distance, through the rarefied air of actuarial tables and columns of statistics—as if looking through an inverted telescope—the claimsman rubs up against life's hard edges. "A desk job. Is that all you can see in it?" scoffs Edward G. Robinson in the 1944 film *Double Indem-*

nity, when Fred MacMurray declines the proffered job. ". . . Just a pile of papers to shuffle around, and sharp pencils and a scratch pad to make figures on, with maybe a little doodling on the side? That's not the way I see it, Walter. To me a claimsman is a surgeon, and that desk is an operating table, and those pencils are scalpels and bone chisels. And those papers are not just forms and statistics and claims for compensation. They are alive! They are packed with drama, with twisted hopes and crooked dreams. A claimsman, Walter, is a doctor and a blood hound and a cop and a judge and a jury and a father confessor, all in one."

In cases from the files of Provident's veteran claimsmen, John Wesley, Leland Fussell, Lewis Emmett, John Starbuck, Floyd Smith and others, sharp pencils often turned into scalpels and bone chisels. Determining the exact cause of a policyholder's demise was sometimes as baffling as it was important to Provident. Millions of dollars might ride on the answer. Was it suicide? Then the company might be liable to return only the premiums paid if the policy had been in force less than two years. Or was it an accident, death by misadventure? If so, the company might be required to pay a "double indemnity," or twice the value of the policy. This question arose in the case of a banker who, while in bed one night, fatally shot himself when he aimed a .45 caliber pistol at his mouth and pulled the trigger. His wife filed an accidental death claim, contending that her husband had had a sore throat and that, half asleep, he was groping for a throat spray on the bedside table and mistook the .45 for the spray. Provident's claimsmen, knowing that juries have been swayed by unlikelier scenarios, set to work reconstructing the banker's last year. Their investigation revealed a failing bank and a history of emotional disorders, information that convinced the wife to drop her accidental death claim.

In cases where policyholders did a disappearing act, the claimsman turned into a blood hound, following the trail left by the policyholder, trying to track him down before the legal presumption of death forced payment of the policy. One such manhunt began in 1966 when a businessman bought a $600,000 policy from Provident and $500,000 in policies from other companies, and then promptly vanished. His car was found near a dam, abandoned but without signs of foul play. Where he had gone from there was anybody's guess. The claimsman who worked the case made more than 170 inquiries across the nation, involved the F.B.I., and after six months managed to flush his quarry, who had assumed a new identity and was living in a distant state.

Apart from the claimsmen, Provident had another effective line of defense against loss: rigorous underwriting standards. Those standards prevented one famous name from entering the list of policyholders. The applicant, a screenstar renowned as a collector of faultless jewels and wayward husbands, signed for a $3 million policy, recommended to her by Provident's agent in Los Angeles. When her application arrived at the home office, it landed on the desk of medical director Dr. William R. Bishop, whose approval was necessary to write a policy of that size. Dr. Bishop, along with his counterparts at other insurance companies, liked to know a little about the habits, healthy or otherwise, of applicants for multi-million-dollar policies. So he ordered a background investigation of the starlet. The background report that came back was a Hollywood press agent's nightmare. Upon reviewing it, Dr. Bishop reluctantly concluded that certain of the starlet's excesses posed unacceptable risks to her life, and Provident declined to insure her.

* * * * *

While the underwriting divisions of the production departments kept risks in check, the executives moved to contain what they saw as a potential threat to the company's existence, national health insurance. Their concern had mounted in 1965 as Congress debated a national health care plan. A cradle-to-grave program would, the executives agreed, cripple the Group Department. But the resulting legislation, Medicare, covered only the elderly. Its immediate effect, Maclellan told the stockholders, would be negligible: "The insurance industry has found that its coverages to those over 65 have been popular, but not generally profitable for the companies. So, the segment of our business that we will be giving up to Medicare is a relatively small segment and a relatively unprofitable one." Still, Congress had issued a challenge that could not be safely ignored. "The possibility that Medicare may be extended to those under 65," Maclellan added, "is entirely a different matter, and one which would be of concern and which should not be minimized. It is, accordingly, incumbent upon the insurance industry to bend every effort to see that there is no need for the Federal Government to enter this field in the case of those under 65. This means we should not only attempt to provide coverage where none exists, but that we should upgrade many of our outstanding plans which now provide inadequate coverages. The Provident, together with the industry as a whole, is committed to this undertaking toward the end of confining Medicare to the small and relatively unprofitable segment of those 65 years of age or older." Not knowing whether the line could indeed be held, management slowed the advance of its most vulnerable unit, the Group Department.

By 1967, Provident's 80th anniversary, the threat of creeping Medicare receded as a more clear and present danger came to the forefront. Inflationary pressures were building in the economy, driving up interest rates and prices. In 1967, inflation, which had been running along at an average annual rate of 1.7 percent since 1949, began a steep climb that would take it to 5 percent in 1969 and to 11 percent in 1974. Salaries and wages rose too, but not as fast as prices. By 1979, a life agent would have to sell $1.5 million of insurance to qualify for the Million Dollar Round Table. And that same year, a $10,000 whole life policy bought in 1949 would be worth less than 3,300 "real dollars." Like the Red Queen in *Through the Looking-Glass,* people had to run faster and faster just to stay in the same place.

For Provident, as for other insurers, inflation cut into profit margins by forcing up operating costs. More damaging still was inflation's effect on whole life insurance, the industry's mainstay. The Great Depression had convinced a generation of Americans that the savings plan built into whole life was a sound and reliable one. It had, after all, passed the test of panic and depression which the stock market and the banking system had failed. By borrowing against its cash value, many had staved off financial ruin during the 1930s. But the spiraling inflation of the late 1960s convinced another generation that whole life was a relic of the past. Its yields of two and three percent were among the lowest, if not the lowest, of any financial instrument. Rather than be locked into this savings plan from the pre-inflationary era, growing numbers of customers opted for term life, which reduced their premiums and thus enabled them to invest the difference in higher-yielding investments, such as certificates of deposit, mutual funds, Treasury bills, and, later, money market funds. The insurance industry's pool of capital had sprung a leak. As Maclellan explained to the stockholders in 1968: "Since 1948, 20 years ago, the life insurance industry has found that its once dominant share of the public savings dollar has dropped from 47 percent to less than 14 percent in 1967. Much of the savings formerly going into permanent cash-value life insurance is being siphoned off by the mutual funds, whose assets now stand at over $55 billion, and have been growing at almost five times the rate of the insurance assets in the past decade."

If more and more of America's savings were going into mutual funds, then, decided Maclellan, so would Provident. Through its subsidiary, PLA Securities Corporation, organized in 1968, Provident began to sell mutual funds through the Life Department's network of agents. The agents had long clamored for this opportunity, recalled one of PLA's organizers, John Witherspoon. "There was so much public acceptance of mutual funds," said Witherspoon, "that many life insurance agents felt their survival depended upon their offering mutual funds as well as fixed-dollar insurance. Many life insurance companies, perhaps most of the large ones, endeavored in some way or other to offer funds to their agents. For some of them this was a very difficult decision because up until that time they had denounced the whole mutual fund concept, had pointed out all the flaws in it and had criticized it; so it meant a very major reversal of their company policy. It was not difficult for Provident to do this because we had never made any statements about mutual funds, either for them or against them. If general agents of the Life Department wanted to sell funds, it was perfectly fine with us. They were running their own businesses." Management never considered the sale of mutual funds as an end in itself; instead, PLA Securities served other, larger purposes. Apart from keeping the agents happy by giving them what they wanted, the "primary reason for entering the mutual fund field," Maclellan explained to the board, was "that this will make it possible to sell a larger volume of permanent life insurance."

To head PLA Securities, senior management selected an up-and-coming officer in the Life Department, H. Carey Hanlin. On joining the company as a $3,600-a-year actuarial assistant in 1948, Hanlin had set his sights on becoming chief actuary one day. But his career took him away from the actuarial work where he felt most comfortable. Encouraged by his friend and mentor Henry Unruh, Hanlin had assumed ever-increasing executive responsibilities, moving up to agency vice president of the Life Department in 1965. Hanlin took charge of PLA Securities while continuing to perform his other duties in the Life Department. Assisting him in managing the new subsidiary were Hugh O. Maclellan, Jr., Thomas Maclellan's great-grandson, who had joined Provident in 1963, and R. Maynard Holt. When interest in mutual funds waned during the early 1970s, PLA became dormant.

Other new investment opportunities beckoned. Under Hugh O. Maclellan and A. C. "Gus" Bryan, the Investment Department entered the field of real estate development. Thus, Provident would act not only as a mortgage lender but also as a partner in the construction, management and ownership of properties across the nation. This arrangement offered a hedge against inflation, since Provident would share in the income from the properties in addition to collecting the usual fixed rate of interest on them. A reluctant landowner during the depression years, Provident was now adding real estate to its portfolio: a shopping mall in Petersburg, Virginia; a medical center in Houston; and the Sears, Roebuck Building in Richmond.

Bryan had joined Provident in 1935 already steeped in commercial lending, and he served the company with distinction in this area until retirement in 1966. Whereas other insurance companies were making F.H.A. or residential loans chiefly, Provident moved vigorously into commercial lending. Bryan enjoyed strong contacts around the U.S., and he developed for the company a sophisticated commercial lending operation. In fact, Provident was one of the first companies in the Southeast to develop commercial lending and compete successfully against much larger companies, owing in part to Provident's ability to respond quickly with an attractive quotation. The company's Investment Department was exceptional in this respect; results from the commercial loans were better than industry averages and with minimal losses. By the time shopping centers became the vogue in the late '50s, Provident was well positioned for leadership in the Southeast in joint-venture mall developments.

The volatile economy also gave rise to other internal adjustments. As inflation pushed operating costs to undreamed-of heights, management recognized the need for a modern system of budgeting. The monthly profit and loss report was a throw-back to a bygone era. Like a weather vane, it told which way the wind was blowing, whereas what the company needed was the businessman's equivalent of a weather satellite, a device that would track expense patterns along a wide front and generate information on which to make a rigorous financial analysis. In 1967, Henry Unruh and Fernand Bonnard, working with William G. Bishop, Jr., designed such a system, known as the Cost Control Program. Put into effect in January of 1968 and frequently refined since, the program would provide, according to Senior Vice President Bonnard, "the kind of information that management needs to measure progress, . . . to see where we are, to measure how far along we are, how we got there, and what needs to be done differently."

The need to do things differently had triggered a name change in Provident's third-oldest department, Railroad, which in 1960 was rechristened the Franchise Department. In insurance terminology, franchise and payorder were interchangeable terms, both referring to the old insurance plans funded entirely through deductions made from the paychecks of workers. As such, the new name signaled no particular change in the department's operation. But it was meant to reflect the intention to branch out beyond the railroads and into other segments of the transportation industry. Ray Murphy, the department's chief, recognized that the railroads could no longer be counted on to generate hefty increases in premium income each year. Faced with a continuing decline in railway employment, Murphy planned to find new sources of income in freight lines and airlines.

*   *   *   *   *

As the 1960s wore to an end, so did the careers of a conspicuously large number of senior executives. In less than four years' time, retirement or death claimed three of the four heads of production departments and two of Maclellan's three executive vice presidents. One of the first to go was Jim Powell, who retired on November 1, 1967. He had accomplished much, taking a weak department and turning it into a powerhouse. Even those who considered him the very devil to work with were quick to give the devil his due. Said one associate, "Jim Powell was an entrepreneur. He built the Accident Department from scratch." And he ran a sizable risk in doing so, added another associate, who said: "The long-term disability business is very dangerous. It is not like life insurance. We know that as far as life insurance is concerned, very few people want to die. They may know that they have a home on the other side, but they are not the least bit homesick for it. In the disability business, if you have over-insured the individual—that is, if you have issued a monthly income benefit which has a high ratio to his take-home pay—then there's always the chance that he may not mind filing a claim and having a monthly income which is not too much less than what he was earning when he was working. As a result, you have to rely very greatly on the kind of agents out in the field who make the initial contact with the prospect. I think we have been very fortunate in the kind of agents we have had in the field, and I think one of Jim's strong points was that he knew how to size up these agents. They really had to pass the taste test as far as Jim Powell was concerned, and you have to give him credit for building up and setting the style that we have in the Accident Department."

Succeeding Powell was Brooks Chandler, who set to work consolidating and augmenting the department's business. Chandler selected as his principal assistant Willard H. Wyeth, a former chief administrative officer of the Paul Revere Insurance Company. Veterans around the department soon began to notice changes. As strong-willed as Powell, if less flamboyant, Chandler had his own agenda for the department. For one thing, he pushed for large increases in non-cancellable business, with the result that premiums from that line increased from $5.6 million in 1967 to $20.4 million in 1972. And he brought order to the bewildering array of contractual relationships with agents, the outgrowth of Powell's fondness for dealing with agents individually and in person. For Chandler, the force of logic counted for more than the force of personality. Although by nature more the technician than the salesman, he nevertheless signed in 1970 one of the Accident Department's largest accounts, the 175,000-member American Medical Association.

In August of 1967 another horseman of production, W. Ray Webb, had preceded Powell into retirement. When Webb came to the Group Department as a clerk in 1924, its premium income totaled just under $900,000. When he left as chief of the department, its collections stood at $182 million, a figure exceeded by only eight of the more than 1,000 companies selling group insurance. To replace Webb, management chose Edward L. (Billy) Mitchell, salesman *extraordinaire.*

For Bob Maclellan, the retirements of Powell and Webb came as a painful reminder that he had a problem on his hands: the graying of senior management. Himself 61, Maclellan knew that he must soon choose his successor. The field of candidates was narrowing quickly, though. Sam Miles, a trusted lieutenant, would be retiring in 1971, and with him would go Ray Murphy, chief of the Franchise Department. Hugh Maclellan, who shared his brother's concern for proper selection of future company officers, wielded influence from his senior executive position in the identification and development of promising leaders.

Although Bob Maclellan was not one to shrink from

exercising authority, neither did he rush to judgment. As he liked to tell his wife Kathrina, "Never trust your own judgment. Get at least two or three other opinions." Following his own advice, Maclellan retained a consulting firm to interview Provident's top executives, size them up, get their views on succession, and report the results. Shortly thereafter, Maclellan reached a decision that he never announced publicly. But according to insiders, he decided that his successor was to be Bill Voigt. Although Maclellan left no record of his intentions, close associates said that he planned to name Voigt president and chief operating officer on May 5, 1969. The 52-year-old Voigt had strong credentials, personal as well as professional. His family and the Maclellans enjoyed a warm friendship dating back a generation. He owned substantial stock in Provident. And he had set a sleepy Life Department on fire, doubling and tripling its business at a pace that aroused the spirit of adventure among the Young Turks, even as older hands advised against the breakneck growth. "It was an exciting time," recalled one executive who had been at Voigt's side during those heady days. "Anytime you grow that rapidly a great many mistakes are made in the agents you are getting. When you add people that rapidly you are going to make mistakes. There were some notorious ones, but these were not fatal to the growth of the department, because it was growing so much that we could afford to make mistakes in people who perhaps did not produce the quality of business that we were interested in."

One trait of Voigt's worried his friends. He found it difficult to say no. His reluctance to turn people down manifested itself in ways large and small. Said one observer: "No matter how much he had to do, Bill would sit and talk to an agent as long as the agent wanted to talk and would discuss any problem, no matter what other things he had to do, and no matter how trivial the problem." As a result, Voigt often ended the day with a backlog of work. It was the pressure of this backlog, said his friends, that caused the debilitating migraines that had begun to lay Voigt low. Some of his associates discussed the situation with Bob Maclellan, who agreed with them that Voigt needed temporary relief from the burdens of administration. Maclellan, accordingly, placed Carey Hanlin in charge of the day-to-day operation of the Life Department, moving Voigt up to direct the overall operations of the Life and Accident departments. But the migraines continued.

While vacationing in Florida toward the end of 1968, Voigt fell ill with what doctors there diagnosed as flu. Feeling worse by the day, he returned to Chattanooga and checked himself into Erlanger Hospital for tests. The results were positive and conclusive: Bill Voigt had leukemia. From Chattanooga, Voigt travelled to Emory University Hospital, where he underwent the latest forms of chemotherapy and radiological treatment. But the disease proved unstoppable, and Voigt died on May 3, 1969.

Shocked and grieved, Voigt's colleagues searched for words with which to describe what they had felt about him. The board expressed itself in uncustomarily strong language, resolving: "The Provident Life and Accident Insurance Company, its stockholders, policyholders, and employees have lost a tower of strength and a great friend in the passing of William W. Voigt." Many remembered him for his human qualities. "You think of him first as a grand person, then as a top insurance executive," mused one staff member. Henry Unruh put the same thought another way when he remarked: "Bill had a great mind and would take great risks to further the growth and profitability of the company. Not everything worked well, and sometimes his trust in the generosity of others was taken advantage of. Bill was kind. I never heard him say anything derogatory of anyone. He was not a pious man, but to me he embodied a true Christian spirit of charity."

*   *   *   *   *

The company closed out the 1960s with triple the assets and premium income of 1959. Expecting more of the same in the years ahead, management proceeded with plans to extend the home office building. The addition, begun in 1970 and completed two years later, harmonized so well with the original that the old and new parts appeared virtually indistinguishable to the casual observer. A tell-tale expansion joint, running the width of the marbled lobby, sutured the two halves together. Like the home office building of 1924, which also combined old and new structures into a seamless whole, this one was a fitting edifice for a company where the traditional and the modern went hand in hand. From a functional standpoint, the addition doubled available square footage. This meant that Provident would have ample growing room until 1990, claimed the consultants who helped with the planning. That turned out to be an overly optimistic prediction. Growing pains were beginning to strike at 10-year intervals, and in 1982 another building would be rising across Walnut Street. But even if Provident continued to outgrow a building a decade, there was land on which to build for decades to come. Pursuing the program of acquisition that his father had started in 1947,

Hugh Maclellan was putting together a plot of some 30 acres that extended for blocks from the Provident complex.

Another plan was reaching fruition, as well. Provident needed a designated successor to Bob Maclellan, who at 63 served as both chief executive and chief operating officer. Maclellan had devoted his life to Provident and, in fact, it was often hard to separate the man and the company. "Bob," his wife would tell him, "sometimes I think I'm married to the Provident, not to Bob Maclellan." It was only natural, then, that he pondered long and hard before placing an executive in line to succeed himself. The long-awaited decision came in March of 1970, when the board ratified Maclellan's choice of Henry Unruh as president and chief operating officer. Unruh was the first man outside the Maclellan family to hold the office of president since 1900, when John McMaster left the company.

Maclellan continued as chief executive and, increasingly, as recipient of manifold honors and plaudits. An honorary Doctor of Laws degree came from King College, in Bristol, Tennessee, and the Chattanooga Kiwanis Club named him Man of the Year for 1970. In May of 1971 *Forbes* spotlighted Maclellan as the executive responsible for Provident's remarkable growth during the previous 18 years. "It's not me, it's all the people around me," the article quoted Maclellan as saying when the interviewer attempted to "put the blame on him for one of the best records in the insurance industry." *Forbes* noted that "with $10.7 billion insurance in force PL&A may be big, but it's also one of the fastest growing, more profitable outfits. Last year, for instance, it earned 11.5% on its stockholder's equity, *vs.* the industry's estimated 9%." The only policy for which Maclellan took credit, *Forbes* reported, was having pushed Provident into the ordinary life business. The article depicted Maclellan as a good deal more than a "caretaker manager," however. "He has an impressive mastery of detail, rattling off reams of statistics from memory, and he has an approach of his own to merchandising: better benefits, stricter screening of customers and, of course, higher premiums." The approach "obviously works," judged the article, which concluded: "Since Maclellan reached the presidency in 1952, PL&A's assets increased eightfold, its insurance in force tenfold. Not bad for a company where all the chief executive does is let other people have their head."

On November 1, 1971, Maclellan turned 65, Provident's mandatory retirement age. But acting "in the best interests of the company and its continued progress," the board made an exception in Maclellan's case, asking him to remain in active service. He consented readily.

In mid-December Maclellan flew to New York to attend a convention of the Life Insurance Association of America, predecessor of the American Council of Life Insurance. On the evening of Tuesday, December 14, he stopped in at a party given by Chemical Bank, then returned to his room at the St. Regis. Next morning, while preparing to shave, he died of heart failure. Provident mourned a strong and honorable leader, a man the Chattanooga *Times* called "a quiet giant in the Chattanooga community."

9

Enter the Technocrats

THREE MONTHS after Bob Maclellan's death, the board of directors on February 7, 1972 elected his successor, or, strictly speaking, ratified the decision already thrashed out by the powerful executive committee. Henry Unruh had emerged as the committee's choice for chairman of the board and chief executive officer. Hugh Maclellan was elected president and chief investment officer. The directors also added another layer to top management, creating the post of vice chairman and general counsel and filling it with Dudley Porter, Jr.

Unruh's election set a historical precedent, for he was the first Provident chief executive without a substantial ownership position in the company. And Unruh had arrived by paths every bit as circuitous as the ones that had led Thomas Maclellan to Provident in 1892. Unruh had grown up among the lower castes who came to his parents' mission in India. He had worked his way through college and graduate school. And he had established himself as an actuary with a Canadian insurer before joining Provident in 1946. Because of his cosmopolitan background and actuarial training, he tended to see Provident less as an institution than as a business to be run along scientific lines.

The sheer size of Provident posed a challenge to any man occupying its top position. The company had grown beyond the point where a single man could reasonably expect to oversee its operations in detail, concluded a study made by the firm of Booz Allen & Hamilton early in 1972. That year, the Group Department alone was several times larger than the entire company had been in 1951. In 20 years' time, employment at the home office had more than doubled, and the field force, now working out of 86 branch offices, had increased from 150 to 720. The study recommended that the number of persons reporting directly to the top man be reduced sharply. Convinced that Provident did indeed have too many Indians and not enough chiefs, Unruh appointed two deputies, Brooks Chandler and Carey Hanlin, and granted them broad powers. Henceforth, the Life, Accident, and Franchise departments would report directly to Hanlin, who as Unruh noted, had demonstrated "an aggressive problem-solving approach." Chandler, as executive vice president for corporate development, would have responsibility for mapping out and launching major campaigns in marketing, planning and acquisitions. The rise of Chandler and Hanlin allowed others to percolate upward in the ranks. Willard Wyeth stepped up to replace Chandler as head of the Accident Department, and G. N. Dickinson, Jr., succeeded Hanlin as vice president in charge of the Life Department.

In his maiden address to the stockholders, on April 15, 1972, Unruh announced another internal shift of consequence: plans were underway to bring Provident's loose confederation of production departments into closer union. As Unruh told the gathering, "Each operating unit is semi-autonomous. In years past we have been so busy in various markets that we have never really coordinated the talents of the company's total human resources. Increased coordination should contribute an additional margin of growth."

To lower the walls separating departments, Unruh sponsored the company's first serious efforts in corporate planning and encouraged a greater degree of marketing cooperation among departments. Directing these initiatives was Brooks Chandler, long an advocate of precise techniques for regulating the company's complex operations. Chandler, working with John Witherspoon and Hugh Maclellan, Jr., put in place a system of planning that involved not only key executives but also middle-level managers, who were given a say in formulating their own goals. By involving people throughout the company, the system avoided, said Witherspoon, "the mistakes that many companies made in building up a large professional planning staff which did the planning apart from the people who were operating the company. Those very elaborate plans are put in nice volumes to sit on the shelf and really don't have much impact on what happens in the company. Perhaps that is just as well, because in many cases those plans are so bad that if anybody did follow them it might lead to corporate disaster."

Unruh's first year in office was noteworthy for introducing another new program, the Management Performance Incentive Plan. Announced on January 1, 1973, the plan offered key executives monetary awards for outstanding performance, as measured by their individual results as well as by the company's overall performance. Like corporate planning and marketing cooperation, the bonus plan was aimed at encouraging teamwork without dampening individual initiative. And while none of these new programs sent the walls tumbling down, their cumulative effect, said one insider, was to "create a sense of the wholeness of the company without destroying the autonomy of the major operating divisions. Unruh still left responsibility in the hands of each department's management, while making all of us conscious that it was important for the whole company to do well, not just the particular part with which we might be associated." Each division continued to develop its own products and sell them through its own distribution channels, a point emphasized by Accident's Dave Fridl, who observed in 1986, "Provident is still the General Motors of the insurance business, selling Cadillacs, Chevrolets and Pontiacs."

Also rolling off Provident's assembly line were capital gains that added up to fortunes for many of the company's long-time stockholders. A hundred shares purchased in January of 1953 for roughly $40,000 had, by the end of 1972, multiplied into 5,600 shares with a market value of some $683,000. And during that 20-year span the shares had paid cash dividends equal to their original purchase price.

Driving this money-making machine was a strong current of income, now swollen to some 2,000 times the size it had been in 1910. Its volume had increased at the brisk rate of roughly 14 percent a year for 62 years. Few other insurance companies could match increases of those proportions. Whether and how Provident itself could maintain the flow were questions very much on the minds of Unruh and his associates. The smooth waters of post-war prosperity had grown turbulent since 1967. Inflation battered paychecks and profit margins. President Nixon's freeze on wages and prices sent storm warnings through the insurance industry, as did the accelerating trend toward a comprehensive, federally-sponsored program of medical insurance. Unable to control the course of national economic and social policy, management could only prepare the company for a period of great change.

Another threat to continued growth came from within the company. As Unruh often pointed out, a large company's rate of growth tends to slow down automatically as its size increases; operations become less efficient, less adaptable to changing conditions. Time and again Unruh cautioned against the sort of smug complacency that causes big businesses to become victims of their own success. In 1973 he told a gathering of life agents in New Orleans: "Just as people develop symptoms of arthritis as they grow older, many institutions, including business institutions, seem to be plagued with this disease as they age. In fact, the disease appears to affect businesses more frequently than it does people. Business arthritis shows up as stiffness, rigidity, lack of flexibility, and a feeling that business must be done on our own terms if it is to be done at all. If allowed to continue unchecked, it leads to a complete inability to respond to major changes and total paralysis."

Unruh and his associates took several measures against business arthritis. For one, they encouraged the free exchange of information and opinion. The company's official statements showed a new frankness and a willingness, as the 1972 Annual Report put it, "to discuss some of our problems as well as . . . our accomplishments." Certain documents formerly kept secret, such as organizational charts, were de-classified and circulated within the company. This more open attitude was reflected, too, in the gradual shift to a more active board of directors. While as a whole the board had rarely deliberated extensively over management's recommendations, individual members had provided valuable guidance. But the meetings became more deliberative as Unruh, Hugh Maclellan and Dudley Porter recruited to the board tough-minded businessmen from beyond Chattanooga who liked to ask hard questions. Among them were W. T. Beebe, chairman of Delta Airlines; Wallace R. Bunn, president of South Central Bell Telephone Company; Dillard Munford, chairman of Munford, Inc.; S. Bradford Rymer, Jr., president of Magic Chef; and Harvey Molé, president of United States Steel and Carnegie Pension Fund, Inc. One result of a strengthened board, noted Carey Hanlin, was to force the chief executive to subject his ideas to healthy doses of self-criticism early on in the process of making decisions.

In another move to stimulate corporate flexibility, management formed two subsidiaries in 1974. These offspring took their parent into unfamiliar lines of business, where it faced the challenge of putting old strengths to work in new ways. One of these subsidiaries, Provident General Insurance Company, offered automobile and homeowners insurance through payroll deduction plans. Briefly, during the 1920s, Provident had ventured into the underwriting of automobiles, only to back out when the losses mounted. Insuring property could be dicey, to judge from the volatile record of earnings compiled by the casualty insurance industry as a whole. But Provident General hoped to beat the odds by limiting its exposure to carefully selected groups of preferred risks.

The other subsidiary traced its origin back to American Republic Assurance Company, a Des Moines-based firm selling variable annuities, an increasingly popular product because it promised inflation-conscious customers higher yields than those obtainable from fixed-rate products. Provident had started developing its own line of variable products, modeling it after the one offered by American Republic. Then the opportunity arose to buy the model, and Provident did, for $5.9 million in cash. American Republic soon transferred its headquarters to Chattanooga, where it was renamed Provident National Assurance Company.

Although Provident National and Provident General represented relatively insignificant portions of the company's business, their formation signified a pronounced shift in corporate strategy. Not since the purchase in 1931 of Southern Surety had management made a similar commitment to new lines of business. And the commitment had been made with full knowledge that these two subsidiaries, still young and unable to pay their own way, would require regular transfusions of capital from their parent. It was a reversal of the unwritten policy that divisions would expand on their own earnings. In the years ahead, Provident National and Provident General would allow the company to market new lines of business outside its traditional ones.

*   *   *   *   *

The ability to open up what Unruh called "new avenues of growth" took on added importance as some established sources of income either played out or else were in danger of being cut off by inflation and governmental action. By far the gravest concern was that Congress would deal the wild card of nationalized health care. The odds of this increased as inflation drove the cost of medical care and insurance beyond the reach of more and more Americans. To some executives at Provident, the National Health Care proposal sponsored jointly by Senator Edward Kennedy and Representative Wilbur Mills seemed to foreshadow the end

of segments of the company's group business. So long
as this threat loomed, management was hesitant to approve substantial investments in the Group Department, which supplied 60 percent of Provident's premium income. The effects of the national health care
crisis were also felt in Wyeth's Accident Department.
With medical costs rising faster than the readiness of
insurance commissioners to grant rate increases, the
department had no choice but to retire its top-of-the-
line major medical coverage. Happily, though, the department had built up other sources of income that
more than offset this loss. In 1975, for instance, it sold
the fifth largest volume of non-cancellable disability
coverage in the nation. And the trend was decidedly
upward. By 1979, Accident would be the nation's number one seller of non-cancellable disability policies.

The Franchise Department had fared less well in
developing alternate sources of income. Under Raymond Murphy, the department had established itself
as a leading insurer of railroadmen. Murphy's persuasive powers with both railroad management and labor
added millions to Provident's premium income. But
by the late 1950s, Murphy realized that the department
was getting larger pieces of a rapidly shrinking pie.
As he knew, contractions in the railroad industry
would eventually put a stopper on Franchise's impressive rate of growth, unless the department diversified
into other parts of the transportation industry. Attempts to win the business of freight lines and airlines
met with limited success, though. Murphy's successor,
B. E. (Ed) Ridge, Jr., demonstrated the same high order
of salesmanship that had made Provident a respected
name among insurers of railroadmen. In 1972, Ridge
and his colleagues negotiated a new contract with the
railway industry's National Health and Welfare Plan,

coming away with substantial gains in Provident's share of the reinsurance. But the airlines and freight lines remained elusive targets. All the while, mergers and layoffs in the railway industry were reducing the department's market there. In 1975 there were 750,000 railroadmen. Ten years later, they had dwindled to 325,000, the population of a medium-sized city. Inevitably, Franchise's rate of growth fell off sharply. Yet the department had sunk such deep roots that even in poor ground it continued to return modest profits.

The staff and agents of the Group Department, like their counterparts in Franchise, showed considerable flair in propagating old business relationships, many of which still thrived after two generations or more. The department numbered among its accounts Consolidation Coal Company, one of whose ancestors, Pocahontas Collieries Company, Provident had first insured in 1898. In the early 1900s Provident agents went down into the mines of the Clinchfield Coal Company to sell insurance. Seventy years later, Clinchfield was a division of Pittston Company, which no longer permitted agents to solicit in its mines. But Provident's agents still solicited at the mines, though now they did so above ground, in the bathhouses where miners showered at the end of their shifts. Other accounts, dating back to the '20s and '30s, included Collins and Aikman, Spartan Mills, Deering-Milliken, Burlington Industries, and J. P. Stevens Company.

The bedrock on which these accounts rested had been formed years ago when the Group Department, then called Payorder, offered to tailor insurance plans to an employer's individual needs, instead of selling the kind of one-size-fits-all plans prevalent at the time. In the years since, the department had expanded without losing touch with its customers or taking them for granted. That, at least, was how many long-time customers saw their relations with Provident. One of these was Walter Montgomery, president of Spartan Mills and a senior statesman of the textile industry. Speaking before a gathering of textile executives and Provident officials in 1974, Montgomery said: "As far back as 1929 Provident wrote the first group hospital-surgical policy in the United States on Carolina Cotton and Woolen Mill at Spray, North Carolina. . . . [At the time] the vast majority of the large insurance companies wouldn't touch a group policy without employer contributions . . . [But] Provident realized and anticipated the needs of textile employees. . . . [Today] Provident insures more textile businesses than all other group-writing insurance companies combined. . . . Why? There are a lot of reasons, but one looms larger than any other. That is service. . . . Service by dedicated people with a genuine interest in the client's needs. . . . Fifty-nine fulltime Provident employees service our business in South Carolina. No wonder we get the kind of service we want. . . . Gentlemen, we your customers salute you."

Montgomery also saluted the man whom he called the textile industry's "very, very good friend," Billy Mitchell. Mitchell was there to accept the salute, but not as head of the Group Department. A coronary condition had sent him into early retirement in January of 1974. He had groomed as his replacement James H. Nelson, a hearty bear of a man with aggressive sales instincts. Nelson filled key posts in the department with forceful salesmen: Philip J. Anzalone, James H. Althaus, V. F. Cooper and Foy Watson. For technical support, Nelson depended heavily on Ted L. Dunn, Thomas J. Johnson, Jr., and Charles Griffith. But all agreed that nobody was capable of stepping into Billy

Mitchell's unique role as the textile industry's "very, very good friend"; nobody, that is, except Mitchell himself. Accordingly, on the request of senior management Mitchell remained active as Provident's emissary of goodwill among his influential friends in the textile business.

Nelson inherited a flourishing department whose premium income placed Provident among the top ten writers of group health insurance, ahead of such nationally known competitors as John Hancock, Mutual of Omaha, and New York Life. Nelson's promotion coincided with the decline of conventional group plans underwritten entirely by insurance companies. As early as the 1960s, a few large employers had assumed all or part of the underwriting liability for their own group plans. The applications and claims generated by these plans were processed by insurance companies at cost, plus whatever profit could be agreed on. Thus the employer insured the plan, and the insurance company administered it. "Self-insurance," as it was known in the trade, allowed the employer to retain and invest the dollars which, had they been channeled through an insurance company as premiums, would have ended up as reserves to cover claim losses. Employers found this feature attractive. Insurance commissioners did not. They took the position that the self-insured employer was evading the legal reserve requirements established to protect policyholders. While the insurance commissioners and the employers were fighting out the issue in court, Congress issued a piece of legislation known as the Employee Retirement Income Security Act, or ERISA for short. Although its avowed intent was limited to protecting the rights of employees participating in pension and welfare plans, its effect, intended or not, was much broader. ERISA contained a provision that effectively abridged the rights of states to regulate self-insured plans.

Freed of regulatory restraint, employers rushed into the insurance business. Before long, Provident and other group insurers saw their underwriting liabilities move upstream to employers; by 1980 some 60 percent of the Group Department's accounts were either partially or fully self-insured. In place of premiums, these accounts generated "premium equivalents" and flat fees. Because it was easier to squeeze profit out of premiums than out of fees, Group's officials would have preferred, in most cases, to keep the liability along with the premiums. But they chose to adapt quickly to what appeared to be a "permanent change in group insurance practices." Said Vice President Tom Johnson: "Self-insurance really took hold among our large customers beginning in the mid-'70s. They started looking at this big wad of money that the insurance company was holding—had to hold—to cover the liability for claims, and began to look for ways to get more economic value out of these funds. We have always taken the position that if something is in the interests of our big customers, we had better find a way to make it in our interests, too. So we decided to get in there and work out arrangements with them to make self-insurance work."

The shift from premiums to leaner forms of income such as administrative fees or premium equivalents put pressure on the department's profit margins. What had been lost in underwriting profits would have to be made up in new business and increased efficiency in administering accounts. The department had long excelled at putting new business on the books. But the administrative function—processing claims and applications—had become as critical to success as sales. In fact, the department's first attempt to enter a lucrative new field, group dental plans, had failed primarily because its manual system seemed to the prospective client incapable of efficiently handling the heavy volume of claims arising from dental plans. Proposals to convert to an automated system had been discussed and tabled. According to Nelson: "We recognized that with the cost of labor going up we had to figure a way to computerize our medical-care payments so that we could get higher productivity and compete with the carriers in other parts of the country who also were computerizing. So in the late '60s and early '70s we recommended to management that we go ahead. Management reached the decision, and we agreed, that with the threat of national health insurance looming we were reluctant to spend a considerable sum, $5 million or maybe $10 million, to computerize. We decided to put it off for awhile and see what happened with national health care."

Then, in June of 1975, the department landed a huge contract to provide dental insurance for the some 40,000 employees of South Central Bell. The bad news was that the contract was scheduled to go into effect on January 1, 1976. This gave the department exactly six months to develop the computerized claims system that it had promised South Central Bell to have up and running when the claims started pouring in. Thus began a crash program, directed by Frank Klaasse and his team of programmers, that produced a working system on deadline. When January 1 rolled around, Group began handling the tremendous volume of small claims with an efficiency that established its credentials as an insurer of dental plans. Other large accounts came Provident's way, including those of White Consolidated Industries, Sherwin-Williams, Mobil Oil and

IBM. Not only did dental insurance boost Group's income but, better still, it opened up opportunities to sell other forms of coverage to some of the nation's largest corporations.

*   *   *   *   *

At the end of 1976 management could take justifiable pride in Provident's performance over the previous five years. Outsiders also took note of the company's strong showing. After comparing the five-year record of the nation's insurers, *Forbes* ranked Provident first in growth in sales and in earnings per share among major investor-owned life insurance companies. In return on capital and equity, Provident ranked second.

The year 1976 also brought a series of retirements at the top. In July, treasurer Cecil Giffen, who in close association with Hugh Maclellan had directed investments, retired after 21 years' service. Giffen's specialty was bonds, while Maclellan gave particular attention to mortgage loans and real estate investments. Named to succeed Giffen and to direct all investment programs was John H. Van Wickler, a newcomer to Provident but a seasoned financial administrator. As treasurer and head of Provident's Investment Department, Van Wickler would manage assets that grew from $1.5 billion in 1976 to $6 billion in 1986. Participation in the ownership of commercial property increased all the while. Begun in the 1960s as a hedge against inflation, investment in shopping malls and office buildings totaled $123 million in 1978. Those policyholders who thought of Provident strictly as an insurer might have been surprised to learn that the company owned interests in shopping malls, apartment complexes and office buildings in California, North Carolina, Tennessee, Georgia, Alabama, Kansas, Mississippi, Florida and

Maryland. Sam Miles, Jr., son of the retired Life Department head, was named to manage this investment area.

In 1971, Provident had ventured into common stock investment programs when such efforts were considered unusual among insurance companies. The management of the Investment Department elected not to rely on outside counsel, but instead to develop its own staff expertise for equities under A. Vincent (Abbie) Keyes. Complementing the success of the real estate and equities programs was the securities division directed by David Fussell, son of retired claimsman and Group executive Leland Fussell. Because of his broad investment experience, Harvey Molé, president of United States Steel and Carnegie Pension Fund, was asked to serve on the board of directors and on the board's finance committee, where his counsel proved to be invaluable. Despite the volatility of financial markets, Provident's rate of return on these and other investments rose steadily under Van Wickler's administration. John Van Wickler nurtured a strong sense of investment discipline throughout his administration, which lasted until his retirement in 1986.

Another change in top management came on November 30, 1976 with the retirement of Vice Chairman Dudley Porter, Jr., Provident's eloquent voice in Washington and Nashville for 27 years. A counselor whose reasoned judgment carried weight, Porter continued to serve as a director, board member and consultant. Named to fill the office of vice chairman was Brooks Chandler, whose formidable grasp of health care issues commanded respect. Chandler's influence extended beyond the trade associations where insurance executives typically held office. In 1971, President Nixon had appointed him as the insurance industry's sole representative on the National Committee on the Health Services Industry, a body which recommended ways of applying the administration's controversial wage-price controls to the health care industry. And in 1976, Chandler was named a member of the American Medical Association's National Committee on the Cost of Medical Care.

On March 31, 1977, Hugh O. Maclellan retired from the presidency, continuing, however, to make his influence felt as a director, member of the executive committee, and chairman of the finance committee. Hugh, like the Maclellans before him, had maintained the family's strong financial commitment to Provident, always valuing Provident above all other financial investments. Just as it had been in 1910, so it was now that the Maclellan family, together with the Maclellan trusts and foundations, held more than 50 percent of the company's stock. The Maclellans had stood by Provident through bad times as well as good. Their continuing support protected against hostile takeovers and left Provident as master of its own destiny. Carrying on the family's tradition of direct participation in management was Hugh O. Maclellan, Jr., a Provident director and senior vice president in charge of corporate planning.

Maclellan's retirement left vacant the office of president. Its new occupant would be in line to become chief executive when Unruh retired in 1979. With that in mind, the board met on April 20, 1977 and, acting on the recommendations of Unruh, Maclellan and the executive committee, elected Carey Hanlin president. Hanlin was the fifth man to hold that office since 1900. But he had been there before. The date was May 1, 1940. The occasion was "Boys' Day in Citizenship," a program through which Boy Scouts were named to civic and business offices for a day. On the appointed date, R. J. Maclellan symbolically handed over the office of president to a 15-year-old Boy Scout whom he had never laid eyes on, Carey Hanlin.

A few years later, as Hanlin returned home following service as a junior naval officer in World War II, Bill Watson, a member of Provident's actuarial staff, called on him to discuss some Boy Scout business. Hanlin declined the request to lead an explorer post, but he accepted his caller's suggestion to consider training as an actuary. The idea appealed to Hanlin, for the work of an actuary involved both math and business, two of his major interests. In 1948, his actuarial degree in hand, Hanlin interviewed with two insurance companies and received identical offers of employment. He chose Provident, though as he freely admits, he did so without any sense of manifest destiny. His rise demonstrated that the interplay of talent, choice and chance was capable of producing fresh variations in Provident's pattern of development.

In the Group Department, as in the executive suite, choice and chance combined to form a surprising outcome, the origin of which dated back beyond the recall of living memory, to the time when Provident's founders began insuring the coal miners of Southern Appalachia. At the time, most established insurers preferred safer risks than those posed by the sort of customer who took a canary to work with him as an early-warning system against an occupational hazard. But where others saw only danger, Provident had seen opportunity as well. Seizing it, the company's founders had built a business on the half-nickel-a-day premiums from miners and sawmill workers. But beginning in the Great Depression, income from coal accounts began to decline in importance. The downward trend continued after World War II, when hydro-electric power dethroned King Coal. Also, much of the insurance once sold by Provident was now provided to miners by the United Mine Workers (UMW) trust fund. Organized by John L. Lewis, the UMW fund was financed out of royalties paid in by operators on tons of coal produced and hours worked. Nevertheless, Provident's agents remained active in the coal fields, selling to salaried workers and also providing unionized workers with coverages that supplemented those available through the UMW plan. Nobody made much of this fact, other than to note occasionally that the coal agents were carrying on a 90-year-old tradition, begun before any of them had been born.

Then, in the winter of 1977, there came a development that combined with this tradition to produce what the Chattanooga *Times* called the "greatest windfall of new business in the company's history." The UMW trust had come under severe financial strain, caused by skyrocketing medical costs combined with frequent strikes that had reduced the royalties coming in from operators. Union representatives demanded that benefits from the trust fund be guaranteed by the coal companies. The Bituminous Coal Operators Association (BCOA) agreed to this, provided that the insurance plan was turned over to commercial carriers. The UMW objected, and eventually declared a strike over this and related issues. In the resulting tug-of-war, BCOA managed to "break" the UMW trust. To insurance companies, this meant that millions of dollars in coverages were suddenly up for grabs. Dusting off their maps of coal country, group insurers rushed in to lay claim to the bonanza. Provident's agents had been there all along, in towns that time had forgot. In many cases, they knew their way around the union halls and hollows better than their competitors. The proof was in the results. When the insurance contracts were awarded in June of 1978, Provident came away with about one-third of the business, covering over 55,000 families. Translated into dollars and cents, this amounted to around $100 million in annual premiums, making Provident the leading insurer in the coal fields. The seeds planted 90 years ago had once again borne fruit.

*   *   *   *   *

As the decade drew to a close, an orderly change of the guard took place. On March 31, 1979, Henry Unruh retired as chief executive, and Carey Hanlin moved up to that position. During Unruh's seven years at the helm, net income and dividends to stockholders had tripled. And Provident's stature within the industry had also risen, partly because of Unruh's work as chairman of the influential American Council of Life Insurance. Of even greater consequence, Unruh had developed a strong team of senior managers, opened up new avenues of growth, sponsored vital initiatives in corporate planning and enhanced cooperation among departments. The principal architect of corporate planning and the formation of new subsidiaries, Vice Chairman Brooks Chandler, retired along with Unruh. To ensure a smooth transition, both Chandler and Unruh remained as consultants to Hanlin. Unruh retained the title of chairman of the board until April 1981.

The internal changes set in motion by Unruh and Chandler gathered speed in the opening years of Hanlin's administration. References to the "Provident family," once a catch phrase around the company, disappeared from the corporate vocabulary, to be replaced by terms such as "participative management," "long-range planning," and "productivity." Cults of personality were discouraged, team work applauded. "We are not the same company we were even five or ten years ago," said Hanlin. "Many once-comfortable assumptions about our industry, government and society are not so comfortable any more." But as Provident responded to these changing circumstances, it evolved along lines established in the distant past.

The company had never been a creature of the marketplace, changing in response to every swing in the mood of consumers, legislators and competitors. Said Hanlin: "Through the years we have been very successful in identifying and developing specific segments of the insurance market which offered good opportunities. We have not tried to be all things to all people, and we will not change that position in the future."

The presence of the past remained strong, even in the midst of experimentation and modernization. In 1983, Provident's ultra-modern West Building rose across from the older building on Walnut Street Hill, creating an architectural study in contrast. The two buildings, radically different in style and separated by a busy street, could have been mistaken for the home offices of separate companies—except for the fact that an aerial walkway of glass and marble connected the two.

The old building was a rectilinear mass of polished marble, monumental in scale, classical in line, and containing a network of masonry walls that compartmentalized the interior space. The offices of the senior executives remained there, but the masonry walls were gradually replaced with hollow walls and partitions that could be easily re-arranged to suit changing needs. Across the street stood the West Building, whose interior walls gave way to a soaring four-story atrium, fes-

tooned with colorful mobiles and topped with a slant-
ing skylight. Provident's cafeteria, center of social life
at the company, moved into this airy space. To enter
it from the old building was to step out of a temple
and into a courtyard. Every working day hundreds of
Provident employees made the trip, crossing the glass-
and-marble walkway that stretched like an umbilical
cord between the old and the new buildings. For many
of them, the two buildings symbolized Provident's
character, anchored in yesterday while reaching out
for tomorrow.

Chronology

1887 (May 24) The Mutual Medical Aid and Accident Insurance Company is chartered by Robert F. Craig, John L. Craig, A. M. Womble, Richard D. Curd and Reuben H. Hunt, who conduct business at 119 East Eighth Street, Chattanooga, Tennessee.

(December 23) The company is re-incorporated as the Provident Life and Accident Insurance Company, whose directors include John Thornton, president; R. H. Hunt, vice president; J. S. O'Neale; M. A. Timothy; Napoleon Loder; J. S. Hunnicutt and A. M. Womble. Until the company begins to issue life insurance policies in 1917, it sometimes calls itself simply Provident Accident Insurance Company.

1888–1891 Directors come and go. Hunt is elected president in 1889. Provident moves frequently, occupying a series of one-room offices: Room 9 of the Montague Block in 1888, 817 Georgia Avenue in 1889, 8 Keystone Block in 1890, and 42 Keystone Block in 1891.

1892 (April 28) Another executive re-organization begins with the arrival of Thomas Maclellan (b. June 7, 1837, Castle Douglas, Scotland) and John McMaster (b. April 3, 1837, Kirkowswald, Ayrshire, Scotland). Maclellan is named secretary and McMaster general manager. The company moves to 531 Richardson Building, located at the northeast corner of Seventh and Broad.

1893 (March 14) $1,031 in profits and $560 in assets have accumulated since the arrival of Maclellan and McMaster. Hunt resigns as president and is replaced by McMaster.

1895 (April) McMaster and Maclellan buy out the other shareholders.

1897   After the Richardson Building burns to the ground, Provident moves its office to the Keystone Building on Georgia Avenue.

1900   McMaster sells his interest to Maclellan and moves to West Virginia, where he organizes a short-lived insurance company similar to Provident. Maclellan assumes the presidency.

1902   The home office moves into the ground floor of the Times Building at 740 Georgia Avenue.

1906   Robert Jardine Maclellan (b. March 26, 1874, St. John, New Brunswick) joins Provident as secretary and treasurer. The office is re-located to the Temple Court Building.

1909   After withdrawing from Alabama and West Virginia, Provident is licensed to do business in Tennessee, Kentucky, and Virginia, where it collects premiums amounting to $108,000 for the year. James Washington Kirksey comes to the company as manager of agents and, later, as chief of the Payorder Department.

1910   (January 31)   Provident raises $150,000 in capital and converts from a mutual assessment company to a stock company, whose officers include Thomas and R. J. Maclellan, Alexander W. Chambliss, Morgan Llewellyn and J. B. F. Lowry. The Maclellans hire two junior officers: William Carl Cartinhour and Leslie Nabors Webb.

1911   Home office moves to the second floor of the James Building Annex. The company enters North Carolina, Alabama and Georgia. Premium income for the year totals $308,000.

1913   Dr. H. L. Fancher is hired as part-time medical examiner.

1914   Provident qualifies to do business in West Virginia, Ohio and Pennsylvania.

1915   Enters Texas, Arkansas and Indiana. 13,000 claims handled during the year.

1916   The Railroad Department, headed by J. B. Cleland, is formed.

(August 5) While vacationing in Manomet, Massachusetts, Thomas Maclellan is struck and killed by an automobile. R. J. Maclellan succeeds his father as president.

1917 (January 1) The Life Department is formed under Albert Caldwell. No policies larger than $5,000 are written unless the excess can be reinsured.

(August) Buys the life insurance business of the Southern Insurance Company, based in Nashville.

1918 (November) Buys the railroad insurance business of the American National Insurance Company, of Galveston, Texas. The influenza epidemic begins, forcing the company to liquidate assets to meet heavy claims losses.

1919 Premium income tops $1 million, and the company is doing business in 14 states.

1922 Thurman Payne replaces Albert Caldwell as head of the Life Department.

(December 28–30) 35th anniversary convention is held at the Signal Mountain Hotel.

1924 Provident moves into its newly constructed home office at 721 Broad Street. The company hires its first actuary, Calvert F. Stein.

(November 1) The Payorder Department writes its first true group plan; that is, a plan funded in part by an employer. The employer is the Tennessee Electric Power Company, and the plan provides group life benefits in amounts ranging from $100 to $1,500.

1926 (April) Purchases the Standard Accident Company, of Detroit. Standard's Harry Conley takes charge of Provident's Railroad Department. As a result of the purchase, Provident enters Iowa, Kansas, Michigan, Minnesota, Montana, Oregon, Washington and Wisconsin.

(June 15) Paul Ray succeeds Thurman Payne as head of the Life Department.

1927 (August 16–18) Provident's annual convention, held in Philadelphia, features a speech by John McMaster.

1928 Robert Llewellyn Maclellan (b. 1906, Chattanooga, Tennessee) joins the company as an auditor in the Life Department.

1929 (April) Acquires the Meridian Insurance Company, of Charleston, West Virginia.

(August) Dr. Charles Henry is named full-time medical examiner. Provident holds its annual convention in Toronto. Premium income totals $5.1 million for the year.

(October 24) The crash of the New York Stock Exchange ushers in the Great Depression.

1931 In addition to R. J. Maclellan, Cartinhour and Kirksey, Provident's board is comprised of Paul J. Kruesi, president, Southern Ferro-Alloys; Thomas R. Preston, president, Hamilton National Bank; Scott L. Probasco, vice president, American Trust and Banking Company; Alexander W. Chambliss, justice, Supreme Court of Tennessee; J. P. Hoskins, president, First National Bank; William E. Brock, president, Brock Candy Company; and John A. Chambliss, Sizer, Chambliss and Kefauver, Attorneys.

(September 1) Provident acquires the accident insurance business of the Southern Surety Company, based in Des Moines. Southern's agency manager, James E. Powell, soon takes over Provident's Accident Department.

1932 Reacting to the nationwide depression, management reduces salaries across the board and slashes other operating expenses. J. H. Leaver replaces Paul Ray as head of the Life Department. Premium income stands at $4.5 million.

1933 On the resignation of J. H. Leaver, R. L. Maclellan takes over the Life Department.

1935   Home office workers receive a bonus of five percent on their salaries. Hugh O. Maclellan, Sr. (b. 1912, Chattanooga, Tennessee) joins Provident. Sam Miles is named agency manager of the Life Department.

1937   (March 15) J. W. Kirksey dies; his responsibility as head of the Payorder Department (now called the Group Department) is divided between Leslie Webb and Howard Hill. Provident's 50th "Golden Jubilee" Convention held at Lookout Mountain Hotel. Provident reports assets of $10 million and premium income of $7.5 million.

1939   Marshall Goodmanson opens the Accident Department's first branch office, in San Francisco.

1941   (January) Harry Conley retires as head of the Railroad Department; Raymond Murphy is named to replace him.

1943   (January) Morgan C. (Joe) Nichols is elected vice president in charge of the Group Department.

1946   Provident adopts the 40-hour work week, and management begins a pension plan for the 343 employees at the home office.

1947   The company begins to acquire land for a new home office on Walnut Street Hill.

   (September 30) Alexander W. Chambliss dies.

   (October 20) R. J. Maclellan announces a new chain of command in which all production departments report to R. L. Maclellan.

1948   Provident qualifies to do business in Canada; its territory also includes 38 states and the District of Columbia.

1951   J. R. Bracewell succeeds W. Keith Kropp as head of the Claims Department. Management names Dr. William R. Bishop to the post of medical examiner, left vacant by the retirement of Dr. Charles Henry. The home office expands into the newly constructed West Building, a five-story annex on Chestnut Street.

March 31   W. C. Cartinhour retires.

(October 17)   A subsidiary, the Provident Life and Casualty Company, is organized for the purpose of doing business in New York.

1952   (January 30)   R. L. Maclellan succeeds his father as president. R. J. Maclellan becomes chairman of the board.

1954   Premiums totalling $61.1 million come from 46 states and Canada.

1955   Provident begins to computerize its manual operations. Sam Miles, vice president in charge of the Life Department, is promoted to secretary of the company; William W. Voigt moves up to head the Life Department.

(March 1)   Treasurer J. O. Carter, Jr., retires and is succeeded by Hugh O. Maclellan.

(October 31)   M. C. Nichols, head of the Group Department, resigns to enter the Episcopal ministry; management selects W. Ray Webb to replace Nichols.

1956   (June 7)   R. J. Maclellan dies.

1957   Total premium income passes $100 million.

1960   (September)   Provident moves into its new home office building at Sixth and Walnut, opposite the Hamilton County Courthouse, on the site formerly called Walnut Street Hill. Company convention held at Lookout Mountain Hotel.

(July)   The Railroad Department changes its name to the Franchise Department.

1962 $100 million in claims paid during the year. The retention limit on life policies is set at $150,000. 75th Anniversary Convention held in New Orleans. Assets reach $269 million. Life insurance in force exceeds $3.9 billion.

1964 Provident reports $5 billion of life insurance in force. Employment at the home office totals 887.

1967 (April 5) Leslie N. Webb dies.

(August) W. Ray Webb retires as head of the Group Department, to be replaced by Edward L. Mitchell.

(November 1) James E. Powell, chief of the Accident Department, retires; Brooks Chandler is named his successor. H. Carey Hanlin is named head of the Life Department.

1969 (March 3) Senior Vice President William W. Voigt dies.

1970 (March 12) Henry Unruh is named president and chief operating officer, while R. L. Maclellan continues as chairman of the board and chief executive officer. Carey Hanlin succeeds Unruh as administrative vice president and chief actuary. G. N. Dickenson succeeds Hanlin as head of the Life Department.

(June) B. E. Ridge, Jr., is named head of the Franchise Department upon the retirement of Raymond Murphy.

1971 (January) Executive Vice President Sam E. Miles retires.

(December 15) R. L. Maclellan dies.

1972 (February 7) The board elects Henry Unruh chairman and chief executive officer. Dudley Porter, Jr., is selected to fill the new position of vice chairman and general counsel, and Hugh O. Maclellan becomes president and chief investment officer. Unruh names two executive vice presidents, Brooks Chandler and Carey Hanlin. Succeeding Chandler as head of the Accident Department is Willard H. Wyeth. Provident expands into an addition to its home office building.

1974 Organizes Provident General Insurance Company, selling automobile and homeowners insurance. Purchases American Republic Assurance Company, later renamed Provident National Assurance Company.

(January)   James H. Nelson is named to succeed Edward L. Mitchell as chief of the Group Department. Following his retirement, Mitchell continues to serve as a consultant to the Group Department.

1976   (January)   Attis E. Crowe is named head of the Life Department upon the retirement of G. N. Dickinson, Jr. The Group Department writes its first dental plan. Home office employment stands at 1571, field office personnel at 919.

(June 30)   John H. Van Wickler is appointed treasurer, succeeding Cecil Giffen, who had held that office since 1972.

(March 16)   William Carl Cartinhour dies.

1977   (April 20)   Brooks Chandler moves up to vice chairman, replacing Dudley Porter, Jr. Carey Hanlin succeeds Hugh O. Maclellan as president. Maclellan retires at 65, but continues as finance committee chairman.

1979   (March 31)   Chandler retires along with Unruh, and the board elects Carey Hanlin chief executive officer. Unruh serves as a consultant until April 1981, with the title chairman of the board.

1980   Provident's board of directors is comprised of W. T. Beebe, chairman, Delta Airlines; W. E. Brock, Jr., chairman, Brock Candy Company; Jac Chambliss, Chambliss, Bahner, Crutchfield, Gaston & Irvine, Attorneys; Brooks Chandler; Robert T. Davis, Jr., president, Dixie Yarns; H. Carey Hanlin; John L. Hutcheson, Jr., retired manufacturer; M. E. Kilpatrick, Kilpatrick, Cody, Rogers, McClatchey & Regenstein, Attorneys; Hugh O. Maclellan; Hugh O. Maclellan, Jr.; Harvey E. Molé, consultant, U.S. Steel and Carnegie Pension Fund; Dillard Munford, chairman, Munford, Inc.; James H. Nelson; Dudley Porter, Jr.; Scott L. Probasco, Jr., president Ancorp Bancshares; S. Bradford Rymer, Jr., president, Magic Chef; Gordon P. Street, Jr., president, North American Royalties; and Henry

C. Unruh. Lowell H. Greene, Jr., succeeds as Life Department head on the retirement of Attis Crowe. Winston W. Walker is named president, Provident National Assurance Company.

1981 David J. Fridl is named vice president in charge of the Accident Department.

1983 A new addition to the Provident complex, the $21 million West Building, is completed.

James H. Althaus is named head of the Group Department.

1985 President Hanlin organizes a senior management team of six people, composed of himself, four executive vice presidents: James H. Althaus, group and health operations; Frederick A. Stoutland, individual life and health operations; Winston W. Walker, pension, mass marketing, and employer-sponsored operations; and Willard H. Wyeth, administrative operations; and Senior Vice President Hugh O. Maclellan, Jr. Heading the production departments are David J. Fridl, Accident; Charles R. Griffith, Group; B. E. Ridge, Jr., Franchise; Lowell H. Greene, Jr., Life; and Thomas B. Heys, Jr., Provident National. Fernard Bonnard and John Witherspoon serve as senior vice presidents.

1986 In partnership with American Healthcare Systems and Transamerica Occidental Life Insurance Company, Provident launches development of a nationwide health care system, integrating the roles of insurer, physician and hospital.

T. Ramon Perdue named vice president of the newly formed Mass Marketing Department.

(June 1) Executive Vice President Winston W. Walker named chief financial officer. Corporate assets exceed $6 billion; life insurance in force stands at $59 billion. Total home office employment stands at 2,738 full-time and part-time employees. Field office employment totals 2,328 people.

Selected Bibliography

Allen, Frederick Lewis. *The Lords of Creation.* London: Hamish Hamilton Ltd., 1935.

____. *Only Yesterday: An Informal History of the 1920s.* New York: Harper and Row, 1939.

____. *Since Yesterday: The 1930s in America.* New York: Harper and Row, 1939.

Armstrong, Zella. *The History of Hamilton County and Chattanooga, Tennessee.* 2 vols. Chattanooga, Tennessee: Lookout Publishing Company, 1940.

Allstate Insurance Company, *Insurance Handbook for Reporters.* np, 1985.

Cahn, William H. *A Matter of Life and Death: The Connecticut Mutual Story.* New York: Random House, 1970.

Carr, William H. A. *From Three Cents a Week: The Story of the Prudential Insurance Company of America.* Newark, New Jersey: Prentice-Hall, 1975.

Carter, John O., Jr. Interview by Jake Wright, 1983. Tape recording, Chattanooga-Hamilton County Bicentennial Library.

Cash, W. J. *The Mind of the South.* New York: Random House, 1941.

Chambliss, John Alexander. Interview by J. A. Chambliss, Jr., 1968. Tape recording, Chattanooga-Hamilton County Bicentennial Library.

Chattanooga Chamber of Commerce. *Report of the Chattanooga Chamber of Commerce, 1889.* Chattanooga: Reynolds & Hickman, 1890.

Divine, Thomas McCallie, ed. *The Wit and Wisdom of Sam Divine: Collection of Sam Divine's Columns from the Chattanooga News 1912–1915.* Chattanooga: Chattanooga *News-Free Press,* 1986.

Eller, Ronald. *Miners, Millhands, and Mountaineers.* Knoxville: University of Tennessee Press, 1982.

Federal Writers' Project. *Kentucky: A Guide to the Bluegrass State.* New York: Harcourt, Brace and Company, 1939.

——. *North Carolina: A Guide to the Old North State.* Chapel Hill, University of North Carolina Press, 1939.

——. *Tennessee: A Guide to the State.* New York: Viking Press, 1939.

Fort, John P. "History of the Provident." Manuscript, 1941.

Galbraith, John Kenneth. *The Great Crash of 1929.* Boston: Houghton Mifflin Company, 1954.

Govan, Gilbert E., and James W. Livingood. *The Chattanooga Country, 1540–1962: From Tomahawks to TVA.* Chapel Hill, North Carolina: The University of North Carolina Press, 1963.

Gurda, John. *The Quiet Company: A Modern History of Northwestern Mutual Life.* Milwaukee: Northwestern Mutual Life Insurance Company, 1983.

Hobson, Arch, ed. *Remembering America: A Sampler of the WPA Guide Series.* New York: Columbia University Press, 1985.

James, Marquis. *The Metropolitan Life: A Study in Business Growth.* New York: Viking Press, 1947.

Josephson, Matthew. *The Robber Barons.* New York: Harcourt, Brace and Company, 1932.

Kennedy, Susan Estabrook. *The Banking Crisis of 1933.* Lexington, Kentucky: The University of Kentucky Press, 1973.

Leuchtenburg, William E. *The Perils of Prosperity, 1914–1932.* Chicago: The University of Chicago Press, 1958.

Lewis, John B., and Charles C. Bombaugh. *Strategems and Conspiracies to Defraud Insurance Companies.* Baltimore: James H. McClellan, Publisher, 1896.

Livingood, James W. *Chattanooga: An Illustrated History.* Woodland Hills, California: Windsor Publications, 1980.

Luther, Edward T. *The Coal Industry of Tennessee.* Nashville: Department of Conservation and Commerce, 1960.

Maclellan, Hugh Owen. "75 Years of Provident History." *Provident Review,* December 1962.

Maclellan, Robert L. "Provident Life and Accident Insurance Company." Address to the Newcomen Society, Chattanooga, 1962.

Maclellan, Thomas. Letters, 1862–1910. Collection of Mr. and Mrs. Hugh Owen Maclellan. Chattanooga, Tennessee.

Martin, Harold H. "Old Dreams—New Beginnings: A History of the Provident Life and Accident Insurance Company." Manuscript, 1980.

McFerrin, John Berry. *Caldwell and Company: A Southern Financial Empire.* Chapel Hill, North Carolina: The University of North Carolina Press, 1939.

McCuffey, Charles D. *Standard History of Chattanooga, Tennessee.* Knoxville, Tennessee: Crew and Dorey, 1911.

McPherson, James Alan, and Miller Williams. *Railroad: Trains and Train People in American Culture.* New York: Random House, 1976.

Moore, William H. "Preoccupied Paternalism: the Roane Iron Company in Her Company Town—Rockwood, Tennessee." *The East Tennessee Historical Society's Publications* 39 (1967): 56–70.

Myers, Margaret G. *A Financial History of the United States.* New York: Columbia University Press, 1970.

O'Donnell, Terence. *History of Life Insurance in its Formative Years.* Chicago: Neely Printing Company, 1936.

Pound, Jerome B. *Memoirs.* np, 1949.

Provident Life and Accident Insurance Company. Board Minutes, 1887–1982.

Provident Review. 1920–1980.

Samford, Frank P. *The First Seventy-One Years of Liberty National Life Insurance Company.* np, nd.

Stone, Mildred F. *A Short History of Life Insurance.* np, 1947.

Tobias, Andrew. *The Invisible Bankers.* New York: Simon and Schuster, 1982.

Wilson, Robert Lake. *Building Stones of Downtown Chattanooga.* np, 1979.

Wiltse, Henry. Manuscript history of Chattanooga. Chattanooga-Hamilton County Bicentennial Library.

Wooley, Bryan, and Ford Reid. *We Be There When the Morning Comes.* Lexington: University Press of Kentucky, 1975.

Index